Continued from front flap]

an approach of more depth than before. Striving to achieve goals of surrealism, depth of psychoanalysis, unity of theme, and completeness of structure, the French critics have indeed created a new literature. Mr. Fowlie believes the change will continue until the philosophical jargon substituting for literary language causes a rigid formalism—and a new literary crisis.

As a comprehensive commentary on criticism ingrained in the French literary world, Mr. Fowlie's historical analysis is for the reader curious about new modes of literary expression, the critic interested in current vistas of his art, and the specialist in criticism and French literature.

Wallace Fowlie took his degrees from Harvard. He presently holds the James B. Duke Professorship of French Literature at Duke University. Recipient of two Guggenheim Fellowships, he traveled in France while researching this book.

Harry T. Moore is Research Professor at Southern Illinois University. Among his recent books are *Twentieth-Century French Literature to World War II*, *Twentieth-Century French Literature since World War II*, and *Twentieth-Century German Literature*.

Other Crosscurrents/Modern Critiques of Interest

For a complete list of Crosscurrents titles, please write to Southern Illinois University Press, Carbondale, Illinois 62901

Siegfried Mandel. *Contemporary European Novelists*

Sergio Pacifici. *The Modern Italian Novel from Manzoni to Svevo*

Harry T. Moore. *Twentieth-Century French Literature to World War II and Twentieth-Century French Literature since World War II*

Frank Rosengarten. *Vasco Pratolini: The Development of a Social Novelist*

Ben F. Stoltzfus. *Alain Robbe-Grillet and the New French Novel*

 *Crosscurrents*/MODERN CRITIQUES

Crosscurrents/MODERN CRITIQUES

Harry T. Moore, *General Editor*

The French Critic
1549–1967

Wallace Fowlie

WITH A PREFACE BY

Harry T. Moore

SOUTHERN ILLINOIS UNIVERSITY PRESS
Carbondale and Edwardsville

FEFFER & SIMONS, INC.
London and Amsterdam

To William and Margaret Wimsatt

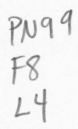

Copyright © 1968 by Southern Illinois University Press
All rights reserved
Library of Congress Catalog Card Number 68–21415
Printed in the United States of America
Designed by Andor Braun

Preface

French literature, massive and complex, has in the last two centuries produced a massive and complex literature of criticism. Although generally concerned with French writing, this criticism is often philosophical, and in a way that becomes universal. In the present book Wallace Fowlie investigates its nature, and it is good to have a work of serious scholarship that is so readable.

He begins in 1549, with Joachim du Bellay's Défense et illustration de la langue française, but he spends only a dozen pages on critics before the nineteenth century. These dozen pages are, however, a valid and important treatment, Gallic in its forceful conciseness. Mr. Fowlie then presents a chapter on "Creative Criticism," ranging from Charles Baudelaire to André Gide and discussing the frequent occurrence, in French literature, of the imaginative writer who is also a critic. He also takes up the professional critics, the men who were critics alone, such as Charles Augustin Sainte-Beuve, as well as the Catholic critics, the existentialists, and others, coming right up to the moment with discussions of Claude Lévi-Strauss and other "structuralists" whose work is so influential today.

Mr. Fowlie's method is one of exposition, analysis, and evaluation. He does little quoting, but his paraphrastic sharpness serves him well in projecting the ideas of all these critics; again he is Gallic in his epigrammatic force. We have long needed just such a book in English.

Henri Peyre has rightly spoken of Wallace Fowlie as the leading American-born critic of French literature. He has written significant studies such as A Guide to Contemporary French Literature, Dionysus in Paris (the modern French theater), The Climate of Violence, and Age of Surrealism, among others, as well as books on individual writers such as Marcel Proust, Stéphane Mallarmé, Jean Cocteau, Arthur Rimbaud, and Paul Claudel. He has also translated the work of many French writers, from Molière to Saint-Jean Perse.

Now James B. Duke Professor of French Literature at Duke University, Wallace Fowlie has taught at Harvard (where he took his degrees), Yale, Bennington, Colorado, and Chicago. He has spent and still spends a great deal of time in France, and as these lines are written he is planning to visit parts of Italy where Stendhal lived. We who are associated with Crosscurrents / Modern Critiques are highly pleased that Wallace Fowlie has written for the series this particular book on French critics.

HARRY T. MOORE

Southern Illinois University
March 21, 1968

Contents

The French Critic, 1549–1967

French Criticism from the Renaissance to the Nineteenth Century

For four hundred years literary criticism has been an integral part of French literature. Critical theory has evolved with literary forms. The poets themselves have often been critics: Ronsard, Malherbe, Hugo. In a few instances, with Baudelaire, Mallarmé, and Valéry, the poets have been the leading critics of their day and of their century. The tradition of criticism is one of the most cherished and one of the most respected in France. From generation to generation, critics, who are often novelists, poets, or dramatists themselves, have defended the rigorous observation of rules and have maintained the excitement of aesthetic theory.

The first important book of criticism in France was *Défense et illustration de la langue française* (1549). It was written by a young man, Joachim du Bellay, who treated the Greek and Roman writers with a fanatical respect. Yet the principal purpose of the treatise was to prove the dignity of the French language equal to the dignity of Greek and Latin. This young poet and critic advised a break with the medieval tradition and a deliberate effort on the part of the new writers to imitate the genres of the classical authors. Tragedies and comedies, following their ancient models of Sophocles and Aristophanes, should replace the *mystères* and *miracles* of the "Gothic" period. Du Bellay was responsible for the love sonnet that was to have such abundant success in the sixteenth and seventeenth centuries, and for the Horatian and Pindaric odes. This early book of criticism was wordy, ill-organized, contradictory, but it provoked enthusiasm and served as a manifesto for two centuries of French poetry.

La Poétique of Jules César Scaliger appeared in 1561 and enjoyed as much popularity as Du Bellay's *Défense*. This work, written in Latin, was the compilation of treatises from antiquity. He compares one with the other, provides examples and definitions, and organizes the vast matter of rhetoric: the rules of tragedy and comedy, the meaning of synecdoche and metonymy, the comparative values of Homer and Virgil. Scaliger's predilection went to the Latin authors rather than the Greeks, and this determined to some degree the shift from the marked Greek influence on the earlier French poets of the Renaissance (Baïf and Ronsard) to the almost exclusive Latin influence on later writers (Montaigne and Malherbe).

The humanist critics were scholars. The tone of their writing was doctrinal. Their comments on literary forms were rigorously compressed into laws. The critics were unsure of their objectives. They were enthusiastic readers of the masterpieces of antiquity, but they seldom went beyond the cataloging of impressions produced by these words. They composed treatises that were the necessary basis for future literary criticism, treatises that were inventories of signs by which ancient masterpieces might be recognized and which might guide the writing of future masterpieces.

The influence of Malherbe dominated the first half of the seventeenth century. His work as grammarian and poet and critic helped to define the precepts of a French art that was to be called "classical" and that occupies the central place in the history of French culture. In a celebrated passage of his *Art poétique* (1674) Boileau was later to hail the advent of Malherbe and the authority of Malherbe in all matters poetical: *Enfin Malherbe vint* . . . Malherbe was the first craftsman in the history of French poetry who discussed analytically and pontifically the rules of his craft. The criticism of Malherbe is to be found in his *Commentaire sur Desportes* where he shows himself the specialist in grammar and the use of words. He denounced erudition in poetry and the unrestrained outburst of lyricism. He purified the French language by narrowing its range and by making it into a language capable of enunciating truths rather than personal passions. Ronsard and the poets of the Pléiade had insisted on loftiness of theme and diction. Malherbe was the first in France to claim ordinary speech for poetry.

Cardinal Richelieu participated in the quarrel over *Le Cid* (1636), but his loyal friend and spokesman, Chapelain, is thought to have been responsible for the writing of *Les Sentiments de l'Académie française sur "Le Cid"* (1637). This work, which occupies an important place in the evolution of French criticism, raises fundamental questions, such as the trustworthiness of the public in judging a literary work. Chapelain develops the theory that the quality of the public's enjoyment of a tragedy, for example, depends upon the author's conformity to the rules of tragedy. His *Sentiments* established the authority of the Académie française on literary matters, and offered the model of a kind of criticism that attempts to base judgment on generalized principles.

The tendencies toward rhetorical bombast and preciosity which developed in France during the sixteenth and seventeenth centuries, largely because of Italian and Spanish models, were opposed by Boileau, whose authority was strong under the reign of Louis XIV. Boileau, Molière, and Pascal, in their critical attitudes, represent a reaction against the spirit of the *salons* and the *ruelles*. Boileau attacked the pedantry of Chapelain, and the French imitation of Italian models. He was backed by La Fontaine and Racine and Molière. Eventually he won over to his side the public and the king himself.

Imitation of nature is the highest rule for Boileau: *Que la nature donc soit votre étude unique*. But this imitation must be carried on rationally, and only in so far as nature conforms to itself, only in so far as nature is universal. Hence, the law of the three unities is applicable because it is natural and reasonable. Preciosity should be condemned because it is unnatural to obscure willfully one's thought by language. Boileau was an artist as well as a bourgeois. He was a craftsman and a painstaking theorist. His defense of reason (*Aimez donc la raison*) established a bond of agreement between himself and his century.

The Quarrel of the Ancients and the Moderns was a complicated affair which transpired during the last years of the reign of Louis XIV. The fundamental issue is still one of controversy: Is man's progress in science and industry perceptible also in the realms of art and letters? In France, this quarrel was the first strong opposition to the Renaissance belief in the need to imitate the ancients. Boileau himself was the principal advocate for the ancients, and Fontenelle, nephew of Corneille and bitter enemy of Racine, was, with the four Perrault brothers, defender of the moderns. For the first time, literary criticism was concerned with the concept of progress. The quarrel provoked sophistry and polemical writings on both sides. Its conclusions centered about the belief that there are other literary models than those in antiquity, that French authors have surpassed Latin authors in the tragedy and novel, and that they may one day hope to surpass them in the ode and comedy.

The controversy stimulated critical opinion not only in France but in all of Europe. It has been claimed that literary criticism in its modern sense originated with the Quarrel of the Ancients and the Moderns. Traces of the leading arguments are found throughout the eighteenth century, in novels and plays. The founding of many newspapers helped to prolong the debate. Pierre Bayle, first of the eighteenth-century philosophers (he died in 1706), to whom Voltaire will owe many ideas, is the free thinker (*libre penseur*) who analyzed for the new century the impossibility of reconciling reason with faith, and who preached the religion of tolerance. He occupies no clearly defined position in literary criticism, but his genius is critical in the highest sense, and his method, which will be his century's, is the search for factual truth.

Voltaire was, without question, the authority in the eighteenth century on literary matters. He was enrolled on Boileau's side and was governed by his deep respect for the rules and examples of French classical art. He praised the English to his countrymen, it is true, but his imitation of *Othello* in *Zaïre* was very limited. After revealing Shakespeare to France, Voltaire became jealous of the glory he had created for the English poet. The eighteenth century demonstrated its major preoccupations in Bayle's *Dictionnaire historique et critique* (1697), in Montesquieu's *Lettres persanes* (1721), and in Voltaire's *Lettres anglaises* (1734). These preoccupations were political, religious, and social. They were not literary or aesthetic, and such works as Voltaire's *Commentaire sur Corneille* remained conservative. During the long course of his career, Voltaire maintained literary criticism at approximately the same point where he had found it.

In a sense, Diderot did more for criticism. At least he attempted more. He seriously questioned Boileau's doctrines of imitation of nature, by claiming that what is natural is not always good. The *Encyclopédie* came into existence largely because of the energy and enthusiasm of Diderot. All of his ideas, from the origin of music to the meaning of the universe, are rehearsed brilliantly in his novel, *Le Neveu de Rameau.* This book is a succinct treatise on the eighteenth century's belief in reason and humanity.

The critics of the seventeenth and eighteenth centuries argued about the application of literary rules but never doubted that the rules existed. Rousseau, who was not a critic by profession but whose literary judgments are everywhere in his books, enunciated the fallibility of criticism and the doctrine of "relativity" that Fontenelle had almost developed at the beginning of the century. The advent of Rousseau helped to bring about the shift from the study of universal or common ideas to the expression of personal or private ideas. He abolished the concepts of literary models, literary recipes, literary rules. His influence was predominant on Mme de Staël, the energetic theorist

of romanticism, and on Chateaubriand, one of the great
stylists of the new movement.

In *De la littérature* (1800) Mme de Staël studies the
multiple relationships that exist between literature and all
phases of civilization: religion, government, customs. In
her analysis of national and racial characteristics, the concept of "relativity" in literary judgment grows in importance. *Le Génie du Christianisme* (1802) of Chateaubriand is not only a work of apologetics, it is a landmark in
the history of criticism. It rehabilitated the Middle Ages
as a glorious past in French national life. In the wake of
Rousseau and Bernardin de Saint-Pierre, it called attention to the color and movement of exterior nature. Chateaubriand claimed that he had replaced the sterile criticism of faults by the fertile criticism of beauty.

Under the influence of Mme de Staël and Chateaubriand, critics began to examine works of art not so much
in themselves but as products of a culture. The danger of
their form of criticism was dilettantism or an expression of
personal preference. This was true of Hugo's famous *Préface de Cromwell* (1827), a kind of manifesto of romanticism, whose ideas had earlier been defined to some extent
in Mme de Staël's *De l'Allemagne* (1810). This book,
with Chateaubriand's *Génie du christianisme* and the systematic historical criticism of Villemain, instituted in
France the study of foreign literatures. But the methods of
criticism underwent the most significant transformation in
the work of Sainte-Beuve who in his analysis of literary
works combined psychology with physiology.

The goal of Sainte-Beuve's gigantic work, which today is
contained in approximately seventy volumes was to infuse
new life into criticism, to enlarge its scope and transform
it. In his short critical papers, collected under the title
Causeries du lundi, and in his long solid works, such as
Port-Royal, he produced criticism which was a review of
French literature in all its forms and which was guided by
a desire to understand rather than to judge. He attempted
to give as full a portrait as possible of the writer under
consideration and raised questions about him which had

hardly been thought of in previous systems of criticism. Such questions included physical and anatomical characteristics of the writer, his educational background, his psychological traits, his temperament as explained by provincial or Parisian mores.

One hundred years ago, Sainte-Beuve was the master critic in France. His weekly article, appearing every Monday, was an important force in shaping literary opinion. He clung doggedly to his own method, although he foresaw the emergence of a new type of criticism that developed in the last part of the century. This type is sometimes called impressionist, because the critics find their criteria in their own judgments and impressions.

Sainte-Beuve did not foresee that one hundred years after the ascendency of his own influence, we would be living through a period in Europe and America when criticism dominates artistic creation, a literary criticism whose form is radically different from his own. Since the days of Sainte-Beuve, some of the major critics have been the major novelists or poets or philosophers: Proust in some of the pages of his novel defines art and its function and the specific art of certain writers; André Gide is critic and aesthetician in the *Journal des Faux-monnayeurs* as well as in the novel itself; Jacques Maritain studies art in the light of Thomism; T. S. Eliot in his theory of the objective correlative proposes an aesthetic principle; Jean-Paul Sartre speaks of the necessity for art to be closely related to the problems of the day.

The criticism of Sainte-Beuve may have little value today if judged by the criteria of the new critics in America, and the new French criticism of Blanchot, Bachelard, Picon, Starobinski, and Jean-Pierre Richard. Historically, however, his position and his method remain important. Because of his work, as it appeared during his lifetime, the public turned more and more to the literary critic for help in reading and in seeing relationships between life and literature.

Under the pretext of historical accuracy, Sainte-Beuve often investigated biographical data of a very intimate nature. The agility of his mind and his intelligence illuminated whatever problems he considered. He is interested primarily in the writer as an individual. He looks upon a book as the expression of a temperament. His judgment of a book is his judgment of the author as a man.

Sainte-Beuve is best when analyzing the background of a writer, or the defects of character in a writer and the noble aspects of his nature. In each essay he offers an impressive documentation in biography and character study and tries to establish general laws that explain various types of minds. This method he applies to major writers (Montaigne and Voltaire) as well as to minor writers (Mme Geoffrin and Grimm). Sainte-Beuve has the curiosity of a psychologist. His method applies better to an explanation of a moderately gifted writer than to an analysis of the genius. The creation of the genius interests him less than the character and the emotions and the personal dramas of the genius. He is constantly trying to discover the characteristics of a man's mind. *La forme de l'esprit* is one of his favorite phrases. But he is hostile to any absolute theory. He experiments cautiously with the data and the facts he has at hand.

The critical method of Sainte-Beuve, fundamentally a moralistic method, resembles no method employed today by the leading French critics. The penetration into the literary work itself by such critics as Sartre (in his long book on Genet), by Georges Poulet (in his recent *Métamorphoses du cercle*), by Jean-Pierre Richard (in his dissertation *L'Univers imaginaire de Mallarmé*) represents another mode of criticism. Each of these critics is distinct in himself (and no one of them occupies the place once occupied by Sainte-Beuve), but together they have created a new intellectual climate, and their work is sufficiently prolific and stimulating to be called the "new French criticism."

The hope of making literary criticism into a science is more apparent in the works of Hippolyte Taine than in those of Sainte-Beuve. His theories of criticism systematized and developed the earlier theories of Mme de Staël and Chateaubriand. As all the parts of an organism maintain necessary connections, so all the parts of a work, or of a man, of a period, of a people, form one system. Each of these systems has an essential or dominant characteristic. Taine proposed to study all the variations of given literary data as influenced by what he called race, environment, and period (*race, milieu, moment*). He looked upon literature and art as the expression of society, as documents awaiting the scholar, the philosopher, and the historian.

Taine developed a method of criticism which was intended to apply to the human sciences the rigor of the natural sciences. It is an elaborate system of causes and laws based upon the belief that art is the result of such knowable factors as race, environment, and historical moment. This theory is owing, in part at least, to writings of Montesquieu, Stendhal, and Michelet. Taine stated the terms of his formula in the preface to his *Histoire de la littérature anglaise* (1864), after developing a detailed example in his book *La Fontaine et ses fables* (1853). A genius is for Taine a product that can be explained by a process resembling a chemical analysis.

During the last twenty years of the century, three academic critics exerted considerable influence. Ferdinand Brunetière, who taught for several years at the École normale supérieure, stressed the moral and social values of works of literature and studied the evolution of literary genres. Jules Lemaître was perhaps the most brilliant of the subjective impressionistic critics. Emile Faguet, who lectured at the Sorbonne, was particularly concerned with elaborating and explaining the ideas of the authors he chose to study.

Paul Bourget's *Essais de psychologie contemporaine* (1883) are still read today. They continue the form of criticism associated with Brunetière, in representing primarily a sociological analysis. He speaks very little about the personality of the authors he studies (as Sainte-Beuve would have done) in order to stress the social value of the work. Literary works are for Bourget the transmission of a psychological heritage. Rather than a critic, he is the historian of French moral life during the second half of the nineteenth century. He denounces a pessimistic turn of mind in his contemporaries which he studies as being the result of dilettantism, of cosmopolitanism, of the impotency of modern love. He concentrates his efforts on analyzing the moral crisis of his age. Literary analysis in Bourget led to social and political analysis. The ten writers he discusses in the *Essais*, including Baudelaire, Flaubert, Stendhal, Amiel, the Goncourts, were chosen, not for the literary value of their writing, but for the influence they exerted on their readers. He approved of Taine's formula: Literature is a living psychology (*la littérature est une psychologie vivante*).

As a writer of critical essays, Bourget has no peer during the last twenty years of the nineteenth century. His temperament of a believer who felt in himself an absence of grace, accounts to some extent for his understanding of pessimism in the writers he studied in his two volumes of essays, and for some of the traits of decadence he analyzed.

At the turn of the century, from approximately the year of Bourget's *Essais* to the First World War, the term "impressionism" occurs frequently in critical circles and quarrels. The word is difficult to define. The dogmatic and scientific type of critic, in the wake of Taine, hoped to reach objective judgments concerning a work of art, but *les impressionnistes* preferred to analyze their own feelings about a work of art. Their criticism was the result of an encounter between a text and themselves as readers. The most resolute of these critics would confess that criticism is a way of speaking about themselves. The goal of this kind of criticism would be the opposite of Sainte-Beuve's, who aimed at analyzing and explaining the subjectivity of whatever writer he was studying.

The impressionist critic is suspicious of any fixed system, of any trace of pedantry, of any rigorous accumulation of data. He looks upon such methods as forms of hypocrisy, of devious ways by which a critic avoids acknowledging that criticism has to come, in the final analysis, from *his* reaction to a literary work. The impressionist wants to preserve the aesthetic pleasure of reading the books he likes best.

There is probably no such thing as a pure impressionist critic. No matter how subjective his writing is, he does have recourse to rules and doctrine and criteria in formulating his critical judgments. Jules Lemaître (with his five volumes of articles, *Les Contemporains*, 1885–1918) and Anatole France (with his four volumes of articles, *La Vie littéraire*, 1888–1894) are examples of critics who believed any objective critical judgment was fundamentally impossible. Their articles resemble stimulating conversations of cultivated men. The merit of a work being criticized is judged by the pleasure it gives. Lemaître reveals his personal taste in extolling those classical works that represent traditional values. He depreciates the symbolists and the so-called decadents who threaten the sense of proportion French classicism means for him. Anatole France does not condemn the symbolists, but he refrains from speaking of them. He seems more open-minded than Lemaître, but he too would preserve the values of the French classical writers.

Remy de Gourmont's criticism appeared somewhat later than France's, since his *Promenades littéraires* were published between 1904 and 1927. His form of impressionistic criticism is quite different from that of Anatole France and Lemaître. He remained close to his period, close to symbolism, to the moment when *A rebours* of Huysmans represented a cult. He defined his own writing as a process of "dissociation," a form of analysis of the ideas in a work of literature where he demonstrated principally a negative tendency, a destructiveness. There is no such thing as absolute beauty for de Gourmont. Every author has his own personality and his own personal conception of beauty which it is the critic's duty to explicate. He follows this principle in his articles on the leading symbolist poets, published in his two-volume *Livres des masques* (1896–1898).

His numerous essays, collected in several volumes, form

a very perceptive record of the thought, the literature, the sentiments, and the customs of the fifteen-year period between 1895 and 1910. The kind of essay written by Remy de Gourmont modified to some extent literary criticism at the beginning of the century. In the history of criticism he appears as an adversary of Brunetière's dogmatism. The critic's role is that of an intermediary between the writer and the reader. De Gourmont accepted neither the rigors of any dogmatic view nor the uncertainties, the wavering qualities of impressionism. There is no one code for the critic to follow, but his taste is sufficient for the development of his writing. He sees the critic's mission as that of helping his generation to overcome prejudice and to recognize the beauty that is being created by the writer. The critic is the creator of art, calling attention to the new beauties of art, and avoiding at all costs the danger of scholarship and pedantry, the temptation to turn his criticism into a treatise on morality or philosophy or justice.

The scholars and the literary historians have been the principal scorners of impressionistic criticism. Their study of a book is the collecting of documents and information that will serve as an elucidation of the book. They emphasize biographical and historical data in order to propose a maximum of objectivity. With the advent of Gustave Lanson (1857–1934) the form of literary history and scholarly research became clearly defined and coordinated. He was largely responsible for replacing a rhetorical somewhat bombastic academic criticism with a "scientific" kind of criticism based upon a minute study of facts, but which always stressed as the goal of literary criticism the forming of the reader's taste and understanding.

Whereas Emile Faguet's articles analyzed the ideas of a writer and his style (a form of criticism which has continued to our day and is often visible in the brief articles of the French literary weeklies), Lanson, obviously influenced by Taine and Brunetière, went much farther in attempting to analyze the conditions that surrounded the work of art and the precise place occupied by the work in literary history. Lanson never denied the subjective elements of his criticism, the personal impression that comes from a direct contact with a work. His importance is in his manner of fusing erudition with criticism, by avoiding a sheer listing or compiling of facts, that never culminates in the expression of an idea or a concept.

To a large extent, the method of research for the preparing of a monograph, promulgated and advocated by Lanson at the Sorbonne and the École normale supérieure, remains in Europe and America the principal method for training young scholars of literature. This method involves the establishment of the text to be studied, an examination of the manuscript and the various editions, in order to provide the text which corresponds the most closely to the intention of the writer. This part of the research is followed by a grammatical stylistic study of the text, involving historical linguistics, vocabulary, versification. The editing of unpublished texts (*inédits*) of the writer often throws light on the main text and on the personality of the author. The establishment of bibliographies helps the scholar in finding books and articles on his subject. A close study of the writer's biography, even the smallest details of biography, will help dissipate legends about the work and the man and illuminate obscurities in the text and in the man's life.

The hunt for "sources" is an important element of Lanson scholarship. They may be found in earlier books of the author or in his biography. Lanson tended to believe that every part of a work had sources that could be tracked down: ideas, phrases, themes. A discovery of the sources of a work will help to establish how an author worked and the degree of originality he possessed. The end of the typical monograph would be devoted to a study of the influences of the work, its posthumous fame, its success in influencing other writers, the place it occupies in the history of literature.

This rigorous scientific method of Gustave Lanson was adopted by a generation of university teachers and scholars.

2

Creative Criticism
From Baudelaire to Gide

The poets of the nineteenth and twentieth centuries, un-hampered by any organized system, such as that of Hippolyte Taine, were critics in their own right. Three at least, Baudelaire, Mallarmé, and Valéry, produced literary criticism which appears today the most vital of their age.

Baudelaire's revelation of poetry revindicated belief in the spiritual destiny of man. His example and his art convinced his readers that man has the right to ask of poetry the solution to the problems of human destiny. His famous poem on symbolism, *Correspondances*, reassigned to the poet his ancient role of *vates* (soothsayer), who by his intuition of the concrete, of immediately perceived things, was led to the idea of those things, to the intricate system of "correspondences." The experience of the poet is the participation of all things invading him, with their harmonies and analogies. They bear the sign of the First Word, of their original unity. In his passages on beauty and on the distinction between art and morality, Baude-laire often speaks of the very special privilege given to beauty to survive moral deficiencies. He certainly believed, with many modern aestheticians, that a blasphemous idea in a line of poetry did not necessarily diminish the formal beauty of the line.

Baudelaire wrote no specifically doctrinal work, no trea-tise that would explain the principles guiding his critical writing on poetry, prose, painting, and music. If he formu-lated anything comparable to a system, it was the warning not to adhere to one system, because of those very characteristics of beauty that attracted him the most: its spontaneity and unexpectedness. Since beauty is not unique, the critic's judgment cannot be unique. His observations and interpretations are at best relative. The beauty of the art of any age in history comes from those elements Baudelaire designates as *particuliers*.

In Baudelaire's earliest example of art criticism, the *Salon de 1845*, he speaks of the artist's function of extracting from the commonplace, from the prosaic aspects of contemporary life, its epic qualities. Théodore de Banville was a friend of Baudelaire, but in his article on Banville (*Art romantique*), he does not hesitate to decry Banville's lofty interpretation of the muse and to claim that the muse has commerce with the living. Art is essentially individualistic for Baudelaire and comes from the inner life of the artist. It is a product of all of his life, but especially of his childhood when the principal elements of his personality were formed.

Baudelaire is only one of several French writers who added art criticism to the main body of their writing, and who practiced this form of criticism with as much sensitivity and acumen as the professional art critics of their day. Before Baudelaire, there had been Diderot in the eighteenth century, and Fromentin, Stendhal, and Gautier in the nineteenth. After Baudelaire, those writers who have contributed to art criticism were influenced by his example and his actual writing: Mallarmé, Valéry, Proust (within the context of his novel), Apollinaire, and André Breton. In pleading the case of Delacroix, one senses that Baudelaire is pleading his own case, especially when he praises the power of melancholy and nostalgia he feels in the large paintings. The words with which he qualifies the painter's art—"modernity," "movement," "intimacy," "spirituality"—can be applied to Baudelaire's poems.

Baudelaire's judgments concerning Flaubert, Hugo, Stendhal, Gautier, Borel, and Balzac have maintained through the years a sturdy kind of validity. But his interpretations of Poe are his major contributions as literary critic. The briefer notices on Gautier, Balzac, and many others, and the lengthier studies of Poe, as well as his excursions into painting (Delacroix), music (Wagner), and philosophy (Joseph de Maistre), mark him as the great critic of the nineteenth century, if greatness is defined in terms of originality and boldness. No other writer of that century, not even Goethe, Coleridge, or Hugo, has left more significant pages on the spirituality of art. Sainte-Beuve, who traditionally is looked upon as the great critic of the age, was too concerned with personality and biography to hold his place beside Baudelaire who was specifically concerned with the work of art.

In reassigning a position of importance to Poe, Baudelaire was seconded by his most brilliant successors, Mallarmé and Valéry. During three generations, therefore, Poe has been read and studied, almost fanatically, by three of the greatest of the French poets. Poe's lecture "The Poetic Principle" was used by Baudelaire in the 1850's as containing the aesthetics of "pure poetry," in which the purpose of art is defined as the revelation of the beautiful. Baudelaire's use of such a text as Poe's "Philosophy of Composition" helped to separate him from a literal interpretation of *l'art pour l'art*, as he found it in the writings of Gautier and Banville, and encouraged him to make more precise an aesthetic belief that is far more spiritual than *l'art pour l'art*.

The sixties was an auspicious decade in Europe; Wagnerian music was for the first time looked upon as initiating a new form of aesthetics, and *Les Fleurs du mal* was having its first profound effects on the spiritual and aesthetic temperaments of the new writers: on Verlaine, Mallarmé, Rimbaud, Lautréamont. Baudelaire was the critic-Narcissus who recognized himself in a painting of Delacroix, in a poem of Poe, and in the polyphony of Wagner. The richness of sound awakened violent emotions in the poet, as the richness of color had once done. The poor reception given to *Tannhäuser*, on its first performance in Paris on March 13, 1861, was offset by Baudelaire's essay "Richard Wagner et 'Tannhäuser,'" appearing on May 4, 1861, in *La Revue européenne*. Although Wagner was more of a mystic than Baudelaire, both men named, as the fearful privilege of the artist, the creation of beauty, and they named beauty the revealer of the infinite.

More implicitly than did even Baudelaire, Mallarmé placed his highest confidence in the sole aesthetic value of a work of art. By this faith, he was the real literary model for such writers as Valéry, Proust, and Gide. Of the necessary solitude of a poet he made almost a religion. No poet more steadfastly than Mallarmé believed that the subject of all poems is poetry, that the reason of all poems is poetry, that the reason for every poem to be written is to become engaged in the creation of poetic language. He saw language as a force capable of destroying the world in order to rebuild the world so that it might be apprehended differently. The title of hero he ascribed to Verlaine might be granted to him in his brave assumption of the state of poet. To be a poet, in Mallarmé's sense, is to engage in a perpetual warfare with oneself. It means the daily destruction of convention, the repudiation of dogma, the removal of all the various assurances that life offers. Being a poet forces a man to a constantly increasing degree of self-consciousness, self-awareness, to a willed exploration of the unknown in himself. The poet is one of those men who each day learn more about their human impermanence without which nothing permanent can be created. These are only some of the critical concepts that can be derived from Mallarmé's writing on poetry and art, on music and the theatre.

For thirty years Mallarmé was interested in those doctrines usually grouped under the heading of occultism, doctrines whose purpose is to discover the structure of the cosmos and the hidden relationships between the parts of the cosmos. Mallarmé believed that the discovery of these relationships comes about in the creative act of the poet. In his essay *Magie* Mallarmé discusses his belief that the original void contained everything in potentiality, even Being itself from which life is born. This life is born in the universe-as-macrocosm, and in man-as-microcosm. In *Notes sur le théâtre* Mallarmé points out that the world is understood and deciphered by man in the metaphors created by the poet. Poetry is a transposition, a true magic that creates another world.

Mallarmé is the most philosophical of all the French literary critics, the most speculative, the boldest in his analysis of what he calls the crisis in literature (*Crise du vers*), in his questions about the value of literature in itself and in its relationship with the other arts, notably music. Mallarmé's thought on his own pages is subtle and difficult to follow. It receives some elucidation and clarity in those writers who follow him and who draw upon him — Valéry, Claudel, and Saint-John Perse; Joyce, Yeats, and Pound outside of France.

In 1895 and 1896, two years before his death, Mallarmé published a series of articles in *La Revue blanche*, under the title, "Variations sur un sujet." Two of these articles, "Le Livre, instrument spirituel" and "Le Mystère dans les lettres," represent a culmination of his thought on the Book, the most mysterious, because it is the most comprehensive, of all the key words in Mallarmé's vocabulary. The alphabet is the one material of the Book, the twenty-four signs which in their innumerable combinations form all lines of poetry. Does a sound have a meaning? Mallarmé never ceased puzzling over this problem. The frequent return in his poetry of certain words is probably explained by the meaning he attaches to the sound. In the swan sonnet, the return of the vowel sound *i* has a piercing quality of light that enhances the monotony of white which is the scene of the poem: "parm*i* l'ex*i*l *i*nut*i*le le Cygne." The negative quality of *n* is implied in such words as: *non, néant, nul, nu, neige, nuit*. In a poem, the words reflect one another, but each separate word contains flashes of light from each of the letters. In a metaphor, Mallarmé explains that a word is a jewel and that each letter is a facet of the jewel.

In his poems as well as in his essays, Mallarmé is the critic scrupulously studying the mystery of poetic language. No one in the history of French letters has explained more fully than Mallarmé this aspect of the aesthetics of poetry. Throughout his life he attempted to purge poetry of elements that are foreign to it. His critical writings are not an apology for hermeticism in his art, but represent a tireless effort to explain how poetry can be brought back to its essence.

Paul Valéry, a self-styled disciple of Mallarmé, continued the critical-philosophical exploration of his master and joined, as Mallarmé had done, the composition of poetry with reflections, of a highly intellectualized nature, on poetry. His writing is more lucid that Mallarmé's, which it often clarifies and justifies. Both of these poets taught, in their critical writing, that the purpose of poetry is not essentially to translate sentiments and sensations. It is the result of thought and labor and technique.

At the beginning of his career, Valéry wrote two short treatises that express his principal ideas on artistic creation, which he would call by the more simple term the poet's work. There is no mystery in artistic creation, he wrote in *Introduction à la méthode de Léonard de Vinci* (1894). Rather than the verb "create," he prefers such a verb as "construct," because the poet uses elements that are at the disposal of everyone. Such a term as "inspiration" is to be rejected. Da Vinci was guided, not by inspiration, but by technical problems and wisdom (*sagesse éternelle*). The second treatise, *Soirée avec monsieur Teste* (1896), is obviously a portrait of Valéry in his search for pure intelligence. He has accepted the concept of the uselessness of any action and any literary creation. Since his mind is able to embrace the entire world, why should he try to re-create fragments of it in art?

When he resumed the writing of poetry, after a twenty-year period of study and isolation, the ideal poet was still for Valéry the disincarnated genius whose intelligence was universal. After the publication of his poems, *La Jeune parque* (1917) and *Charmes* (1922), he became a public figure, and was, until his death in 1945, solicited from every side for articles, prefaces, commentaries, and judgments. He himself chose the articles which make up the five *Variété* volumes (1924–1944) and which form the best of his critical writing. He excels in deriving general critical theories from his study of specific works. The poet's technique, for example, based on restrictions and freedom in poetic creation, is the subject of his study of *Adonis* of La Fontaine. In his essays on Stendhal, Baudelaire, Verlaine, and Mallarmé, he analyzes the relationship between an author and his work in order to discover whether the readers understand a work as the author had understood it.

In his two Platonic dialogues, *Eupalinos* and *L'Ame et la danse* (1923), Valéry is concerned with the material constraints and obstacles that are present at the birth of an artistic work and that explain to some extent the art. In *Eupalinos* Socrates and young Phaedrus converse. It is a debate in which Phaedrus expresses his belief that in the creation of beauty the artist's senses and body are important, but Socrates emphasizes the artist's pure intelligence. The same two debaters are in *L'Ame et la danse*, where dance is defined as that art which teaches man to understand his physical bodily movements, as poetry is that art which teaches man something about the power of currently-used words. In watching a dance, which is achieved by calculation and exercise, Phaedrus admires the dancer's body and what she tries to represent in the dances, but Socrates enjoys the intellectual fervor that comes to him from watching the perfect execution of the dance.

Valéry's criticism is always the reconstruction of some spiritual adventure initiated by the work he is considering. He is fully concentrated on how his mind reacts to a given work. But he tries first to understand the secrets that explain the construction of the work, its functioning, because he wants to reconstruct the functioning of the mind that was responsible for the work. *Valérysme* has come to signify in France the study of the human mind. The simple facts of biography will have little value for such a critic as Valéry. He came to believe the author is not the cause of the work. Rather the work creates the author, and it behooves the critic therefore to focus his attention on the work.

Valéry never separates critical thought from creative activity. In speaking of his own poetry, he used to say that his only interest in it was the stimulation it provided him for reflections about the poet. In his critical pages, he always returns to the problem of how a work was written and how he could characterize the mental process by which the art was created. Especially in his pages on Mallarmé, he emphasizes the need for the critic to feel and demonstrate deep sympathy for the work he is criticizing. By sympathy, in the fullest meaning of the word, the critic is able to penetrate the mental world where the work had its birth.

Whenever a work is being written, there is inevitably, according to Valéry, to some degree at least, an awareness of a future public, of an audience to whom the work is being directed. In other words, no one has ever written a line solely for himself. This element, this invisible presence of a reader, Valéry calls charlatanism. It is an element of impurity that exists in every literary production, and the critic has to remember the existence of this impurity. That is why it is impossible to explain fully the man by the work. It is also the reason why it is impossible to explain fully the work by the man. The work leads back, not to a man, but to a mask. *Il ne faut donc jamais conclure de l'oeuvre à un homme—mais de l'oeuvre à un masque—et du masque à la machine.* This important hypothesis is discussed by Valéry in *Tel quel I, Cahier B 1910.*

Total sympathy for the writer and his work would be disastrous for the critic, because he would thereby be reduced to silence. Sympathy does not mean the critic's identification with the creative artist's mind. It means on the part of the critic an effort to define the mind and a

confronting of that mind with other types of minds, with
other types of geniuses. From this kind of study, the critic
derives useful lessons. Bémol, in his book *La Méthode
critique de Valéry*, calls this method an egotistical criticism. The ultimate goal of the literary critic is, for Valéry,
the discerning of differences between the type of rhetorical writer, comparable to the leader of a street brawl who
controls the crowd for a moment, and the other type of
writer who slowly reaches a position of power and imposes
his work as an enduring empire. The first type of writer is
the destructive revolutionist. The second is the type of
writer who creates laws (see *Tel quel I, Cahier B* 1910).

Charles Péguy founded his *Cahiers de la quinzaine*
(1900–1914) in order to convert the public to his principles, and he grouped around him men who were guided
and inspired by his thought: Romain Rolland, André
Suarès, Daniel Halévy, Julien Benda (for a short while),
and others. They were moved by Péguy's heroism, by his
violent criticism of critics and professors. He was indefa-
tigable in defending his ideas in pamphlet after pamphlet.
In his praise of Hugo and Corneille and writers of antiquity (see *Les Suppliants parallèles*), he defined himself
and the fervent generosity of his ideas.

He associates the perils that beset the modern world
with the practice of and the belief in rationalism. The
philosophy of Henri Bergson is, for Péguy, the antidote.
Bergson came to tell us that passion is not obscure and
that reason is not clear. In attacking what he calls the
"scientific method" of literary criticism, he derides the
habit of the critic (as he sees it in Taine's study of *La
Fontaine et ses fables*) of never staying close to the text
itself, of always moving outside of the text, to some
vaguely defined beginnings. He attacks the so-called scien-
tists of literature for never discovering within the text its
meaning (see *Victor-Marie, comte Hugo*, 1910).

Not one of the *Cahiers de la quinzaine* could be looked
upon purely as literary criticism, and yet Péguy's work,

and the books he sponsored, contributed important elements of criticism. Péguy was probably the only *normalien*, the only student of the École normale supérieure, the only student of the rue d'Ulm, to show unequivocally the spirit of the École normale supérieure, the only one to show open hostility to the traditional form of humanism represented by the school. He contributed more than anyone else to making Gustave Lanson into a scapegoat, by ridiculing the methods of erudite scholarship. The publication of the *Cahiers* and the discussions carried on by the writers in Péguy's group, revived some of the oldest debates in French literature: the antithesis between Corneille and Racine, the opposing philosophies of Voltaire and Rousseau, the concept of France as reflected in the writings of Michelet and Hugo.

A professorial academic type of criticism had flourished before Péguy, in the work of Brunetière, Lemaître, and Faguet. Péguy was responsible, to some degree at least, for its decline. The symbol of the academic *fauteuil* was derided by Péguy who used the symbol of the more simple *chaise* to represent a more basic, more earthy set of values. The diverging points of view, represented by Péguy and Barrès during the first decade of the twentieth century, go far beyond literary criticism, but they involve literary criticism and count in the history of those ideas which are reflected in the writings of the critics. The divergence has its roots in the Dreyfus case which became essentially a controversy of intellectuals. It forced them to take sides in the fight over values. The literary-intellectual phase of *L'Affaire Dreyfus* began with Gabriel Monod's report which pointed out a judicial error in the verdict of the trial. Monod was a history professor at the École normale supérieure, a center representing the impartiality of historical criticism and the value of precision and accuracy of which the French mind has always been proud. Zola's letter *J'accuse!*, published January 13, 1898, in *L'Aurore*, instigated the movement of the "intellectuals" who demanded a review and a revision of the case.

Péguy was one of the young *normaliens* who took sides

with the *dreyfusards*, while Barrès aligned himself with opponents of Dreyfus who called themselves *La Patrie française* and who were ultimately defeated. Out of *La Patrie française* arose *L'Action française*, a right-wing royalist movement where the influence of Charles Maurras was added to and surpassed that of Barrès. Three writers in particular looked upon themselves as defenders of French tradition and engaged upon a campaign of nationalistic criticism: Maurras, Barrès, and Léon Daudet. They were militant critics, especially Maurras, who spoke vehemently against the methods of psychological and historical criticism. They opposed romanticism as being a force of corruption in French civilization, and advocated a return to the classical tradition which they called the one true tradition of France.

In his book on George Sand and Musset (*Les Amants de Venise*) Maurras denounced the upsetting influence of romantic emotions. Daudet was more vituperative still, in his attacks on the romantic aberration (see *Le Stupide 19e siècle*, 1921) of which he saw traces everywhere, in Sainte-Beuve, Taine, Lemaître, Anatole France, in naturalist writers and symbolists also. In all fairness to Daudet, it should be pointed out that he was one of the first critics to believe in the genius of Marcel Proust.

Pierre Lasserre's attack on romanticism (*Le romantisme français—essai sur la révolution dans les sentiments et les idées au 19e siècle*, his doctoral thesis, defended at the Sorbonne in 1907) was a more sober and a more reasoned attack than that of Daudet, but he too judged romanticism as the disintegration of French culture. And he too accused Lanson of founding a literary science where taste does not count. In a series of essays, collected under the title of *Jugements* (1923–1924), Henri Massis continued the tradition of Maurras and Lasserre, in the sense of writing criticism that was essentially the denunciation of the modern mind.

His earliest attack, written in 1911 in collaboration with Alfred de Tarde under the pseudonym of Agathon, was entitled *L'Esprit de la nouvelle Sorbonne* and was a continuation of Péguy's criticism, in that it denounced the Sorbonne as being the fortress for Dürkheim's sociology and Lanson's method of literary history.

Patriotism and Catholicism were joined in the polemical writings of Massis under the double aegis of Barrès and St. Thomas Aquinas. After studying at the Sorbonne, he allied himself, through friendship and common interests, with Péguy, Maritain, and Ernest Psichari (Renan's grandson). His was one of the many religious conversions among the intellectuals about 1913. His second book, written with Alfred de Tarde and published in 1913, *Les Jeunes gens d'aujourd'hui*, was widely read at that time and received with enthusiasm by those who were its subject.

Among the several literary magazines founded before 1914, and in which those writers destined to become major literary figures published their essays and critical writings, *La Nouvelle revue française* stands out as the most significant. The high quality of the first issues in 1910, under the direction of Jacques Rivière, attracted the attention of the new writers. Rivière's own literary criticism was collected under the title of *Études* (1912). As editor, he was responsible for the publication in the *Nouvelle revue française* during 1910–1914 of the works of those who were to become major writers in the period between the two wars. In the pages of the magazine a veritable criticism of criticism was carried on. The first collaborators, grouped around André Gide, had written for the last symbolist magazine, *L'Ermitage*, and were determined not to found, with the *Nouvelle revue française*, another literary school, but to pay more attention to technical literary problems than to moral issues in the works they criticized.

All of Proust's early writings were exercises or preparatory drafts for the final work, *A la recherche du temps perdu*.

In a passage of the fifth part, *La Prisonnière*, where Marcel listens to the playing of Vinteuil's septet, he realizes that all the earlier compositions of Vinteuil had been timid essays, preparations for the triumphant septet, which uses the earlier compositions and themes, develops them more fully, and represents the entire life of the composer. In the same way, the early writings of Marcel Proust all flow into the final novel where they are deepened and transformed: the short stories and sketches of *Les Plaisirs et les jours*, the novel *Jean Santeuil*, and the critical work *Contre Sainte-Beuve*. The critic and the novelist are fully apparent in *A la recherche du temps perdu*, but to them has been added the aesthetician, the artist who has come to a profound understanding of his method, of his subject matter, and of the philosophical meaning of art.

Among the manuscripts and notebooks discovered fifteen years ago, in the possession of Mme Mante-Proust, niece and heir of Proust, the suite of articles and essays, edited by Bernard de Fallois under the title *Contre Sainte-Beuve*, serves as an admirable introduction to the aesthetics of Proust. Although the writing of this essay was begun in 1908, it is associated with conversations Proust had with his mother prior to her death in 1905. He began the writing of an article on Sainte-Beuve for *Le Figaro*. Several months later, the article had grown to three hundred pages. The title *Contre Sainte-Beuve* is justified by Proust's discussion of Sainte-Beuve and his hostility to the critical method of Sainte-Beuve. There are instances of personal memories in the essay, portraits of friends and artists, notes on reading and art. Most of these pages, rewritten and transformed, will find their way ultimately into the novel.

In his many literary studies Sainte-Beuve never separated the writer from his work. He believed that the literary art is explained by the man who did the writing, and he accumulated all the necessary factual information he could concerning the writer he was criticizing. He consulted correspondence, questioned friends and witnesses, read diaries and history. Proust looks at Sainte-Beuve as initiating the historical-biographical method which Taine was to refine by emphasizing *le milieu, le moment, la race* of whatever genius he was attempting to explain.

A large part of Proust's novel is spent in denying the reliability or the accuracy of such information. The self which a man shows in his daily habits, in his social intercourse, in his vices is not, for Proust, the real self. It is a superficial self, a mask, induced by habit, by a routine of daily living, by the many constraints society imposes on all of us, by hypocrisy and cowardice. Proust is concerned, as was Bergson, with the inner, realer self, *le moi profond,* which is alive in dreams and in very privileged states of consciousness.

Sainte-Beuve had scorned or neglected four nineteenth-century writers whom Proust was to place among the greatest of the creative spirits of France: Nerval, Baudelaire, Balzac, and Stendhal. He had personally known Henri Beyle (Stendhal) and had easy access to the kinds of information so important in the application of his critical method. Yet Sainte-Beuve judged all the novels of Stendhal as "frankly detestable." For Proust, this was a blatant error in critical judgment, and for this and other reasons he castigated the biographical method of the critic.

Proust, in his treatment of the composer Vinteuil in *A la recherche du temps perdu,* and of the painter Elstir (whose work is more fully analyzed than that of Vinteuil, although no element in it is used so often as the "little phrase" of the sonata), looks upon a major work of art as a new beginning in the history of art, as a form in itself not dependent on previous forms or theories. The individuality and even the originality of the artist are emphasized in the novel as making a unique contribution, a world in itself, which, once again, explains the world.

In the last part of the novel, *Le Temps retrouvé,* when the protagonist is in the Hôtel de Guermantes, Proust develops, in close relationship with the narrative, his fundamental theories on literary criticism and aesthetics which form one of the most illuminating exposés in twentieth-century criticism. The protagonist Marcel has just made the discovery that a work of art is the life of the artist and that there is a record of this life deposited in the deepest part of himself. He calls it an inner book, *un livre intérieur*. The only one able to read this book, to decipher it, is himself. It is comparable to Mallarmé's *grimoire*, the conjuror's book of magical recipes, of apparitions that can rise out of a secret ordering of words. The material of the work of art is therefore intact at all times. The labor of the artist is a painful deciphering, a difficult transcription into words of what has been recorded in his psyche—*ce livre, le plus pénible de tous à déchiffrer.*

Marcel learns as a corollary of this principle, that the artist is not free to choose the subject matter of his art. The art he creates is predestined by the life and the character of the artist. What is imperative in the case of the authentic artist is the need to pass beyond the superficial daily self and to discover the true self which is the container of the past. Proust looks upon a great work of art as that unity which destroys the illusions forming our faulty comprehension of life. Art is the solution of every human problem for Proust.

The novelist Bergotte, in the novel, is the type of man able to make himself into a mirror and who therefore is able to reflect all of his life and all the events that have taken place around his life. It is of no consequence that this life of the writer, as Proust says, is mediocre and commonplace. What is important is the reflective power of the novelist, his ultimate value as mirror. If this hypothesis in the aesthetic system is granted, then any accusation of immorality will have no basis. In countless passages of his novel, Proust fuses his critical reflections into the narrative. Theory and story are used to support one another because of the kinds of questions that Marcel, the protagonist who wants to become a writer, asks himself: What is the relationship between life and art? What is the meaning of a work of art?

An example of a serious exaggeration made by critical scholars is the influence of Bergson on such writers as Proust, Péguy, and Thibaudet. During the five years that preceded the First World War, 1908–1913, when Proust wrote *Contre Sainte-Beuve* and *Du côté de chez Swann*, Bergson did not exert the influence that has been claimed, and Freud and Kierkegaard were not read in Paris.

All of André Gide's writings can be considered as basically critical. He was a critic in the narrower sense when he wrote out his reflections on the books he read and developed his theories on the literary arts in articles, prefaces, and lectures which have been collected in various volumes: *Prétextes, Nouveaux prétextes, Incidences, Divers, Dostoïevsky, Interviews imaginaires.* Wherever he traveled, in France, Italy, Africa, he related in his *Journal* observations on the books he read and reread. He has recorded a multitude of literary judgments which he often returned to and revised. They form today nothing comparable to a treatise or a unified book, but they represent views and convictions of a truly critical mind in the highest sense, because Gide's literary criticism is closely allied with his moral criticism, with his analysis of human values. The clearest expression of the so-called Gidian values is often to be found in his critical writings.

Gide called himself an *être divers*, a man basically opposed to any system. His criticism of Christianity is largely in terms of his rejection of religious authoritarianism. To reach the ideal of sincerity, man has to be free and available to all experience (*disponible*). His discipline comes from within himself. Moral problems are never absent from the writings of Gide, neither from his *récits* (*L'Immoraliste, La Porte étroite*) nor from his essays or *Journal*, but the purpose of a work of art is never for Gide that of proving or instructing or improving. One sentence of his in particular is still remembered for its castigation of edifying literature: "Bad books are made from noble sentiments." (*C'est avec les beaux sentiments qu'on fait de la mauvaise littérature.*) He believed that the critical powers of the artist are at the source of great art. A great artist has to be a critic first, because art is opposed to the conventional, to those criteria that are admitted by the majority. The critical spirit in the writer makes him into the unusual man and creates out of his literary vocation a force that is irresistible.

Gide returned often to a certain number of critical concepts that today are associated with his name. He never neglected an analysis of the work of art itself that he was studying, but he was always drawn to the makeup of the artist, to the physiological and psychological deficiencies in a man that account, at least to some degree, for the quality of the work. At the basis of any reform, of any revolution, whether it be political or religious or literary, Gide sensed the presence of some disorder, of some lack of equilibrium, of what St. Paul called a "splinter in the flesh."

He believed that a literary work is best characterized, not by the tradition it supports and reflects, but by the newness it exemplifies, by its freshness and novelty. The work is done by one creator, with individualistic traits. A single man's understanding of his own humanity is the mark of the literary work that will distinguish it from all others. The genius of a race is manifested in the genius of a single writer. Dante, Shakespeare, Molière, Dostoïevsky reached that highest degree of universality in their writing because they were primarily observers of their own individualism, bent upon reaching the fullest expression of what was human in themselves.

In his discussion of Mallarmé (*Prétextes*, pp. 117–21), Gide considers the poet as an example of the difficult artist who, by the quality of his work, seemed to scorn the general public, but who created slowly through the years a small public able to understand him and eager to esteem him. The general public is perilous for the artist, because it is bound to force him to facile conventions. Every example of great art is originally attached to one moment in history, and to a transitory élite of that moment.

The special journal Gide kept as he wrote his major novel, *Journal des Faux-monnayeurs*, is one of the illuminating critical pieces of the twentieth century, a veritable treatise on the art of the novel written by a practicing novelist as he was composing his novel. Gide was sensitive to the crisis the novel was going through in the twenties, and the need to reexamine the traditional form of the novel and to discover new approaches that would be more in keeping with the development of science and psychology. He argued in the *Journal* that a fully determined structure of the novel should give way to something resembling the fortuitous happenings in life, to the innumerable beginnings of dramas that never reach completion or solution. Gide saw the art of the novel as a permission given to the novel to narrate the accidental associations of life. The necessity for an action—the beginning, the middle and the concluding of an action—should not be imposed on the novel.

In the *Journal des Faux-monnayeurs*, Gide speaks of his resolution never to profit from the momentum a given chapter creates. The following chapter should start up afresh without the need of continuing and maintaining the intrigue and impetus of what preceded it. Therefore a novel should not be inevitably an arranged story. It should be, rather, a meeting place, a crossroads (*un carrefour*) where several ways or habits of life come together, where characters, who have nothing in common, encounter one another.

Gide's critical stand, especially in terms of the novel, is clear in this short succinct tract. Long before the theories of the new French novelists in the 1950's, he advocated the abolishment of the clearly defined plot and a drastic reduction of detailed psychological analysis of characters and of description of places. He used another device for the construction of his novel: the introduction of the novelist himself as a character of the book. This strategem permitted him an easy way of commenting on the art of the novel, on analyzing, not a situation in the novel, but the metaphysics of novel-writing.

The history of literary criticism taught Gide that what is admired today in major works was not admired by the contemporaries of the writer. It is an almost inevitable law that a great work of literature at the time of its first appearance will encounter opposition and incomprehension and suffer by unjust attacks. This is because new art is characterized by elements of surprise. The novel is freer and more lawless than other forms of art. It lends itself best to this law of surprise where, within the story, as in life itself, every element becomes a new point of departure, where nothing is concluded once and for all.

Today the position of Gide in French letters seems as assured by his critical writings and theories as by his creative works which in many cases are explicitly allied with critical theory. In his role of critic, as well as of prestigious literary figure, he fought hard for the revindication of freedom in many domains. He supported the ideas and the claims of the youth of his day and helped to launch several of the younger writers: Saint-Exupéry and Henri Michaux, among others. His translations of Joseph Conrad (*Typhon*, 1923) and his study of Dostoïevsky (1927) helped to introduce French readers to foreign literatures. His treatment of characters, especially in *Les Faux-monnayeurs*, showed them as acting in accordance with their freedom and the logic of their own temperament. His practice of the novel cannot be separated from his aesthetics of the novel and from his position of moralist.

3

Professional Critics

Julien Benda looked upon himself as the guardian of the French rationalistic spirit. Reason is the faculty in man that will permit him to discover and establish stability in the modern world where everything seems directed against reason, according to this critic. By opposing all the new tendencies and ideas of his age, Benda appears today as a totally isolated figure. He invented the character of the *clerc*, of the rationalist, insensitive to passion and determined to defend abstract ideas. His first attack, at the beginning of the century, was waged against Henri Bergson and Bergsonian thinkers whom he believed responsible for the decline of French stability and solidity in the domain of ideas and art (*Le Bergsonisme ou une philosophie de la mobilité*, 1912). The same kind of attack is made in *Belphégor* (1918). The idol Belphégor is the source of confusions and emotions who has encouraged intellectual laziness in the modern age by inducing the reader to commune with a writer rather than understand him. Intuition has supplanted intelligence.

In *La Trahison des clercs* (1927) Benda defines the mission of his *clerc*, namely the thinker, as that of fighting for ideas, and particularly the ideas of justice and truth. These ideas could lead a man politically to the left or to the right, but they must lead him toward order and social progress. *La France byzantine*, published after the liberation, in 1945, is an attack against those modern writers who, according to Benda, indulge in facile effects and in errors of logical reasoning. The attack is continued in

Trois idoles romantiques (1949), where Benda opposes Proust as the novelist of intuition, and Claudel as the poet exalting natural man.

The great evil for Julien Benda is irrationalism. He sees it expressing itself, on the political plane, in the myths of instinct and passion, in the use of such words as race, class, state. On the artistic plane, he sees it in the obscurity of modern poetry. Rationalism alone is suitable to the essence of man and to his dignity. The genius of this critic has been spent more in denouncing than in showing how rationalism can be restored. His temperament is aggressive and violent. He is a powerful writer, an authentic writer, and totally hostile to other writers of his age. His criticism is obviously that of a strong temperament. He himself does not possess those qualities of the ideal critic. His most brilliant passages, written in defense of what he calls rationalism, are his denunciations of Bergson, Péguy, Gide, Proust, and Claudel, and they are precisely the passages that seem today the most devoid of any lasting critical acumen.

Albert Thibaudet, who died in 1936, was the last of the major French critics in the twentieth century whose critical method remained close to that of the nineteenth century. His position is midway between the scientific scholar and the impressionistic critic who publishes a weekly or monthly chronicle. In explaining a work of the past or of the present, Thibaudet tries to place it in perspective, in a *vue d'ensemble*, and in his best pages, he illuminates a work and restores it in a new vision. Thibaudet's training in geography and history and sociology is visible in his efforts to classify a writer by his generation and his province. He was one of the first critics to study Mallarmé (*La Poésie de Stéphane Mallarmé*, 1912; revised edition, 1926), and his book has not been invalidated by the countless studies of Mallarmé since that time. The same can be said of his *Flaubert* (1922). A still later book, posthumous in fact, *Réflexions sur le roman* (1938), contains detailed judgments on novelists who are no longer read, but many of the generalities about the novel are striking and provocative. Thibaudet's power of renovating a subject and seeing it in a new and stimulating way gives its value to his *Histoire de la littérature française depuis 1789*, published posthumously in 1936.

For twenty years Albert Thibaudet regularly contributed the principal literary criticism to *La Nouvelle revue française*. Each of his articles is characterized by solid documentation and by a sensitive and vigorously stated reaction to the work in question. Thibaudet's particular skill was his fusion of information concerning a work and his intuitive understanding of it. He was never dogmatic in his estimates and judgments. He was guided by curiosity and a great eagerness to understand. No French critic has possessed greater clarity of vision than Thibaudet in pointing out currents and movements, themes that define an age in literary history, impulses and enthusiasms that characterize a given generation.

Thibaudet became practically the official French critic between 1920 and his death in 1936, by reason of the regularity with which he wrote in the *Nouvelle revue française* (these were the great years of the magazine) and by his constructive criticism when he often indicated in his articles suggestions to the writer he was judging. The philosophy of Henri Bergson is the principal clue to Thibaudet's critical method. He attempts to understand and explain the creative impulse that continues throughout the work of a writer and that best characterizes the writer. In the book on Mallarmé, for example, he devotes most of his time to a study of the origin and the evolution of the poet's metaphors. Bergsonian philosophy, about which Thibaudet wrote a book, *Le Bergsonisme* (1923), deeply influenced his thinking about the art of criticism, and led him to replace the facile departments or divisions in the work of a writer with a study of the continuing movements throughout the work. He applied his method in his book on Flaubert and thereby opposed the more traditional criticism on Flaubert which tended to classify the novelist's works as either "romantic" or "realist." As a Bergsonian, Thibaudet chose to look upon a major writer as a world in himself rather than as a part of a world.

Thibaudet was one of the first French critics to investigate psychoanalysis in terms of literary criticism and to estimate what psychoanalysis could bring to our understanding of literary works. In *Physiologie de la critique* (1922) he distinguishes between three kinds of criticism: that of scholars, that of creative writers, and that form generated in spontaneous speech. He concludes that no one form represents an ideal type of criticism.

Thibaudet's art is a combination of several critical methods. He can appear as philosophical as Ernst-Robert Curtius does in his *Balzac* and as psychological as Bellessort does in his *Balzac*. He can emphasize the techniques of the writing in question or literary history. Alfred Glauser in his book, *Thibaudet et la critique créatrice* (1952), has clearly defined Thibaudet's position as that of forerunner of the new criticism in France.

The critic first has to feel sympathy for and understanding of the book he is criticizing, and then describe it in terms of its genre and tradition, and place it in terms of its generation and its province. Thibaudet probably suffered from writing too much and with too much regularity. He organized an article quickly and ingeniously and never failed to create striking formulas for his reactions. His erudition was such that he could improvise easily and demonstrate a virtuosity that was not always profound. In his cavalier attitude toward surrealism, he showed in his last years an unwillingness to accept and study new forms and new techniques of writing.

André Suarès, a good friend of Gide's and for many years closely associated with the literary group of *La Nouvelle revue française*, defined the critic as the man not essentially a judge but one who seeks to understand a work of art and then to communicate his understanding. The ideal critic for Suarès would be Montaigne or Stendhal, writers who experienced passions of all kinds, and whose imagination is a highly developed faculty of their nature.

Suarès is the master of a form of criticism that is a literary portrait, one achieved by a series of brief colorful and peremptory remarks. His essays are celebrations of the exceptional type of writer, the creator of characters, or the type of tragic poet able to infuse life into ideas and sentiments: Dostoïevsky, Cervantes, Tolstoy, Pascal, Baudelaire. The critic is also a creator, for Suarès, whose writings are rich in psychological insights, who has to relive all the experiences and passions in the books he considers. Suarès is critical of Sainte-Beuve for remaining too close to biographical anecdotes and failing to explain the real greatness of the work. The method of Taine is quite specifically castigated by Suarès: the accumulation of *fiches*, so elaborate a system of note-taking that the dominant ideas and form of a work always escape him.

Like Suarès, Alain is more a critic of ideas and customs than specifically a literary critic. His collections of short pieces, *Propos*, do contain literary criticism but only incidently. At several points in his writings, he expresses a lack of tolerance for the typical critic and the hope that he will not be classified with the critic. But he is also distrustful of abstract philosophy, and tends therefore to use such a writer as Balzac as a starting point for his own ideas. He needed the company of great writers, he needed to feel admiration for those writers who stimulated his thinking and aroused in him a desire to mount to their level. Admiration was a mental attitude for Alain. Effortlessly he embraced the ideas and the type of mind of the writer he studied. His temperament disliked the kind of criticism that was hostile and derogatory. It is too easy to find defects in a writer. The challenge of the critic, according to Alain, is to discover new beauty that has not been felt or analyzed before him. Alain taught a generation how to read with curiosity. He gave the example of a man eager to establish a dialogue between himself and the writer whose work he was reading. It was the kind of dialogue that led him in the opposite direction from scholarship and history.

Alain illustrates an extreme form of impressionistic criticism. The work in question, whether it be Balzac or Montaigne or Valéry, serves the critic as a means for expressing his own reflections, his own philosophy. His typical *propos*, a two-page commentary, starts with a specific detail and moves toward a generality. The original detail would be a personal experience of Alain's on a remark from Stendhal. *Propos de littérature* (1934), for example, is a collection of separate commentaries from which, however, generalities concerning art may be derived. Alain sees the origin of art as coming from passion and delirium, but it is always disciplined by the thought of the artist and by the hardness of the medium: by marble, if the artist is a sculptor, by the laws of versification, if the artist is a poet.

His commentaries on *Charmes* and *La Jeune parque* of Valéry (1929 and 1931), his book on *Stendhal* (1935) and his essay *Avec Balzac* (1935–37) have little interest for today's readers of Valéry, Stendhal, and Balzac. But his writing was a source of stimulation for the generation who read him and for many of those young Frenchmen who were his students. His intelligence was Cartesian in its close examination of all those dilemmas and difficulties that might block the way to man's search for truth. Alain believed that the noblest calling of man was the creation of a work in which he created himself.

Paul Léautaud was probably the most self-centered of all the twentieth-century French critics. He praised only those writers whose ideas and temperament and animosities coincided with his own. Whenever there was any trace of what he deemed a bourgeois prejudice in a book, he denounced it vigorously. He was attracted only toward those writers whose spirit, like his own, was belligerent and quarrelsome. This trait is so marked in Léautaud that it can be questioned whether he was a critic in any sound sense.

He knew intimately the theatre from an early age. His theatre criticism, published regularly in *Le Mercure de France,* in *La Nouvelle revue française,* and in *Les Nouvelles littéraires,* has been collected in two volumes under the title *Le Théâtre de Maurice Boissard.* It is a moody, irritable, and irritating kind of criticism, a campaign against facile romantic effects in writing, an exposing of the critic's own phobias, an attack often on the personal moral deficiencies of the writer rather than on his literary defects. It is criticism with intermittent digressions on the critic's own life, on his love of cats and dogs, and other extraneous themes. And yet Léautaud's critical writing often has penetrating observations on the authors he studies. In his theatre criticism he was often the first to point out weaknesses of dramatists who no longer are esteemed. His admirations were few. Among the dramatists, he praised Molière and Shakespeare, and scorned the Greeks, Corneille, and Racine.

At the death of Jacques Rivière, in 1925, Jean Paulhan assumed the direction of *La Nouvelle revue française,* and this function of his critical spirit has probably served the cause of French letters more than his actual critical writing. In 1941 he published a mysterious little book entitled *Fleurs de Tarbes.* The origin of the title was a sign Paulhan had seen at the entrance to the public garden in the Pyrenees town of Tarbes forbidding anyone to carry flowers into the garden. This sign became for the critic a symbol of contemporary literature where writers tend to go beyond their traditional role of creators of books destined to divert and distract a public. Today's writers easily turn into philosophers and moralists, into confessors and leaders. The readers in their turn become difficult judges of the writers and demand from them evidences of sincerity. The public grows skeptical of the careful writers, of the stylists whose language seems a disguise for their thought. And thus, the new writers give up their stylistic effects and write spontaneously and easily in order not to be judged as "precious." They are not allowed to enter the garden of letters with flowers, with anything that might attract their public. This is the image that represents for Jean Paulhan a reign of terror in literature which he wants to see end.

He points out in *Fleurs de Tarbes* the uselessness of much of the critical writing where critics rarely consider the works themselves and where they follow too closely nineteenth-century theories. As the critic tends to become historian or psychologist, the writer's work—the poems or the novels—is neglected or forgotten. Paulhan is harsh, often justifiably so, when he claims that in criticism of his day the work to be criticized has given way to a study of the writer, and the writer has given way to a study of the man. He wants the critic to demonstrate an interest in the way a writer uses language. He urges that the literary critic renounce the vast problems of philosophy and science and face the problems of language which he as a writer should not avoid. Paulhan is distrustful of theses and hypotheses. For him, the critic is an investigator, a man who inquires into the state of language and the use of language.

Nothing is left to chance in the carefully and modestly worded *Fleurs de Tarbes*, where Paulhan points out some of the distressing contradictions of modern thought, contradictions which he calls *la terreur*, and which could also be called a crisis in literature. The essay is concerned with the divorce between the writer and the public in the twentieth century, with the ever-increasing number of critical doctrines, with the writer's dilemma of whether he should consider himself a god or abandon the art of writing and self-expression. Writing is an artifice, and today's writer is puzzled over whether he should consider it a supreme exercise of the mind or a game in which he can have no confidence and no belief. Has language become a devaluated product, a set of rhetorical devices no longer adequate to express and sustain its message? Paulhan, with the skill of a penetrating essayist, has pointed out the abyss that exists between the inner truth a writer finds within himself and the transmission of that truth into what has to be conventional language of common-places and clichés. Paulhan's own career illustrates the drama he describes: that of a man growing so suspicious of the words he has to use that he ends by becoming incom-municable and silent.

If there is a remedy for such a crisis, it will have to be the discovery of a new faith in language, the discovery of a new relationship between thought and language. To avoid the facile tricks of verbalism, the writer will have to redis-cover the sincere power of the word. The reality of poetry is perhaps to be found in its very contradictions. In Paul-han's essay *Clef de la poésie* (1945), a continuation of *Fleurs de Tarbes*, he studies the seeming contradictions between poetry as sound and poetry as symbol. One attri-bute does not necessarily cancel out the other. Sound and meaning are both necessary.

In his literary judgments, the critic Thierry Maulnier reflects the strong anti-romantic bias of Maurras and the equally strong pro-classical bias of Valéry. He took this stand early in his career in his book on *Racine* (1936) and in his long essay on poetry in *Introduction à la poésie française* (1939). In order to understand Racine, he un-dertakes an interpretation of his tragedies almost in a theatrical sense. After a very penetrating study of the nature of poetry, Maulnier distinguishes two great centu-ries of French poetry: the sixteenth and the twentieth. These affirmations are made in a series of striking formu-las. His criticism is almost a manifesto. His vehement praise of Maurice Scève and Robert Garnier and Racine is to some degree a way of disqualifying much of contempo-rary literature. His principal thesis is stated and restated with total conviction throughout his writings: Poetry is primarily a question of language. He tends toward a predi-lection for hermeticism in poetry and preciosity. In his earlier criticism, Maulnier expressed his approval of seventeenth-century politics, but in a later book, *Violence et conscience,* he acknowledged the validity of the Marxian criticism of capitalism.

In the 1930's Maulnier's book on *Racine* and Robert Brasillach's study of *Corneille* (1938) represented the point of view of younger critics eager to claim the greatness of the sixteenth and seventeenth centuries in French literary history, and to define the masterpieces of those centuries by their alliance with monarchy and religion and with a rigorous aesthetic conception, of which romanticism and much of modern literature will represent a differing aesthetic. Their attack was mainly against the nineteenth century and recalled the earlier similar attack of Léon Daudet. Even if their attack seems ill-founded, they did rehabilitate a few of the great seventeenth-century figures who had lost much of their freshness by having been submitted for so long to the codifying tendencies of schoolteachers and the scholastic analyses of professors.

4

Catholic Critics

The principal trait of Charles Du Bos is the intellectual
and spiritual sympathy he expresses for the authors he
studies. He quite literally communes with his authors in a
manner that is almost passionate and, to a degree, almost
an identification with them. A feeling of admiration for
the authors being studied and a closeness of spirit to them
are indispensable for the kind of criticism Du Bos writes.
He calls it an approximation, because any total understanding is impossible. He tries progressively, slowly, to
understand the work. By close analysis of passages, by
comparisons with other authors, and by the high-lighting
of significant details, Du Bos attempts to understand the
object of his attention, which is always the human mystery in an author, that basically ineffable part of his nature
expressed in his work.

The title of his seven volumes of essays, *Approximations*, published between 1922 and 1937, describes his
critical method. His reading of a book was an achievement
in its own way, because the reading was so profound and
intuitive that he could at times, as in the case of Proust's
novel, prophesy what was to come in later volumes. He
was often a close friend of the author he wrote about, as in
the case of Gide, and the pages he devoted to the work
seemed to be a conversation with the writer. His criticism
is a form of personal journal, and his *journal* is made up of
reflections quite worthy of figuring in a book of criticism.
If Du Bos is, to some extent, a panegyrist in his *Approximations*, he is also meticulous in his attention to the

chronology of a writer's work, to the influences on a writer, to the recurrence of words in his texts which often reveal predilections and fantasies.

His conversion, or what he preferred to call his "formal adherence to Christianity," took place in 1927. Ten years later he taught for one year at the University of Notre Dame in Indiana. He possessed an extensive knowledge of English literature (his mother was English) and a taste for a psychological interpretation of literature. It was not quite psychoanalysis, but something close to the practice of writers with whom he felt an affinity: Bergson, Proust, Gide, Jacques Rivière.

The religious conviction of Charles Du Bos is quite clear in his essay *Qu'est-ce que la littérature?* published just before the war in 1938. It defines literature as an incarnation, as a creation to which life owes its survival. The aim of literature is to provide pleasure, to provide consolation for sorrowing human nature, and even to offer a cure for the illnesses of mankind. We are helped when we read the books of the greatest writers and realize that they suffered from the same ailments we suffer from. Literature is that art in which a man may take full conscience of himself.

For Du Bos the great works of literature are in the empyrean, and the act of reading them is an ascent, almost an assumption. It is the site of the archetypes. In those works human nature has been given its highest, its purest expression. They are free from contingencies. They are the fixed stars and their light through the centuries continues to illuminate men.

This very lofty interpretation of literature has been shattered today by Jean-Paul Sartre, especially in his work bearing the same title as Du Bos's, *Qu'est-ce que la littérature?* The two opposing views have been analyzed by Jean Seznec in his inaugural lecture at the University of Oxford, in 1952. Quite justifiably, Seznec points out that this opposition between Du Bos and Sartre is symptomatic of the crisis of modern thought. The problems it raises go very deeply into the new or renewed view of literature as expressed by such a critic as Ortega y Gasset, who believes that modern man has lost respect for the past, and by Paul Valéry, who claims that life and death have lost their significance, and by André Malraux, who, long before Sartre, spoke of the feeling of guilt that writers feel today.

And yet, the thesis of Du Bos is one that may in time be more lasting than Sartre's. It claims that great literature is always aiming at the fixed stars because a work of literature must be attuned to the nature of the human mind rather than to the nature of any given society.

Jacques Maritain has a great affection for clarity of thought, for the limpid formula, for the expression that appears purely rationalistic. But he does not avoid obscurities when the subject calls for them. His long cohabitation with mystics and poets has taught him many lessons on the ultimate ineffectualness and inefficiency of language. He is attracted by the enigmas of man, by the most troublesome and the most persistent enigmas. Maritain's thought is accessible to all, but to gain access to this thought requires initiation to many subjects and especially to Thomism: both the philosophical assumptions of St. Thomas and the powers of synthesis in Thomistic thought.

Maritain's is the vocation of the philosopher, that of being a witness of the world in its meaningful presence, and of welcoming the world by means of a language that attempts to reveal the truth of the world. Early in his career, *Art et scolastique* surprised simultaneously two worlds in Paris: the philosophers and the artists, the students of philosophy and the students of art. Both worlds realized that the author of this book was a metaphysician who seemed to look upon himself as if he were a contemporary of St. Thomas as well as a man who had meditated for a long time on the paintings of Rouault, a revolutionary and totally modern artist.

The principal ideas of *Art et scolastique*, which first appeared in 1920, were examined by Maritain in *Réponse*

à *Jean Cocteau* (1926), in *Frontières de la poésie* (1935),
in *Situation de la poésie* (1938), and in *Creative Intuition in Art and Poetry* (1953). In these five works,
Maritain exposes his understanding of aesthetics under
two general headings: the theories about art expressed by
the scholastic philosophers, and the mysterious characteristics of contemporary art, especially in the realms of
painting and poetry. Maritain's task was made difficult
by the absence of any solid treatise on art by a scholastic.
But in choosing and collecting the many disparate and
scattered statements about art in the writings of St.
Thomas and other medieval philosophers, he exemplified
as a writer the skill of integration which is one of the
characteristics of St. Thomas himself. The study of
medieval art, as well as the study of certain texts of St.
Thomas, taught Maritain many lessons on the artisan, on
the dignity of the artisan's craft, and prepared the way for
the philosopher's understanding of the artist and of what
he will call the sublimity of the artist's vocation.

The relationship between art and morality was one kind
of lesson discussed in *Art et scolastique* with exceptional
thoroughness and objectivity. When he approached the
immediate and specific problems of the modern artist, this
philosopher-aesthetician wrote as one who felt deeply and
personally the spiritual problems of his day, those which
since the Renaissance have made the artist into an un-
happy and, at times, desperate man. Maritain has not only
studied the psychology of the modern artist, in contrasting
it with the spirit of the medieval artisan, but he has also
studied countless examples of modern art and the laws
that seem to govern these works. These studies have
helped him in his understanding of modern man and the
tragedies of modern history, in the social and political
sense. The exaggerations and the inhumanity of the political state are not without their counterpart in the drama of
the modern artist.

In claiming that poetry must always remain within the
realm of art, namely within the limitations of something
to be made, something to be created, he expresses at the
same time fear for such a poet as Arthur Rimbaud, for

example, who attempted to pass beyond the natural frontiers of poetry, who experienced the temptation of knowledge, of changing his being, of discovering a dialectic and a form that would ultimately efface poetry and silence the poet. In his moving analysis of the angelism of Rimbaud, Maritain defined and redefined the rules of art and the temper of the artist, but he also expressed, with the feeling of an artist himself, the spiritual drama of this dilemma and its relationship with the general spiritual anguish of modern man.

From his knowledge of Thomistic thought, Maritain was able to point out the dangerous pretentions to "purity" which certain schools and forms of modern art have made. He described the significance of this purity, the peril it implies in the artist's seeking to reach a state of independence from morality. In a passage of *Art et scolastique*, in which Maritain considers examples of the modern novel, he outlines a theory, or rather a measurement of guidance for the modern writer, when he stresses the importance of the understanding and spirituality of the artist himself when he treats the problem of evil. It is the famous passage on Proust, whom Maritain would like to have seen endowed with the perceptiveness of a St. Augustine when he approached certain themes in his work. By this kind of striking alliance, Maritain analyzes the confusion of aesthetic and ethical values which he looks upon as one of the besetting plagues of our age.

In his long career as a writer and thinker, Jacques Maritain has often expressed gratitude for the debt he owes to other writers and to friends. To Henri Bergson, first, who was perhaps the leading master for Maritain in his early years. To Charles Péguy he owes especially the sense of the temporal vocation of the Christian. A third debt of gratitude, and perhaps the heaviest of all, is to his godfather, Léon Bloy. The prophetic vocation of Bloy has been continued in Jacques Maritain. Bloy spent much of his life in denouncing the lukewarmness, the fears, and the prevarications of today's world. Maritain adapted the affirmations he found in Bergson, Péguy, and Bloy to the affirmations of faith he studied in St. Thomas.

The lesson he learned from St. Thomas was the method he has faithfully applied to all of his work: *distinguer pour unir,* the need to distinguish carefully all the elements of a problem in order ultimately to unite them. With every problem that Maritain has touched, he ends by fusing into an organic growth the supernatural life of the Church and the temporal life of the world. His humanism neglects nothing concerning God, because it is based on the double conviction that man is made from nothing and that man is made in the image of God.

Because of the many grievous dilemmas that Maritain has attempted to solve, his writing can seem at times to be a form of lamentation, a sorrowing poetic expression. But then it can change abruptly into a vigorous energetic form of polemics where passion is married to poetry thanks to his knowledge of scholastic philosophy. If his thought derives from St. Thomas, his position today as a philosopher is quite independent. The university world and the Catholic world have both come to realize this independent stand of the French philosopher. This stand is luminously apparent in his most recent book, *Le Paysan de la Garonne: Un vieux laïc s'interroge sur le temps présent* (1966), which is an attack on many idols of the day and is reminiscent of Maritain's first book, *Antimoderne* (1922).

Whether he is speaking of Christian philosophy or of modern aesthetics, the accent of Maritain's voice is personal. The transparency of purity of his style lead one to believe that his nature is both that of a philosopher and a poet. All his life he has been a reader of the poets, and his perceptive comments on the work of Baudelaire, Rimbaud, and Cocteau are among the most precious he has bequeathed to future students of French poetry. Maritain knows and accepts the great claims of poetry: It is the essential language; it comprises the fullest extent of human expression; it is the absence of speech as well as the written word.

Daniel-Rops (pseudonym for Henri Petiot) was a prolific writer in many genres: journalism, the essay, the novel, religious history. As a religious thinker, all of his writings are efforts to show that religion is still a force in the world and not incompatible with ideas directing today's civilization. *Notre inquiétude* (1926), is a long essay on attitudes and psychological problems of French youth in the 1920's. In his later years, his vocation of historian (he was the youngest *agrégé* in France, in 1922, at the age of 21) won out over his earlier vocations of essayist and novelist. When he was elected to the Académie française in 1955, he was an acknowledged historian of the Church, with such works as *Jésus en son temps* (1945), *L'Église des apôtres et des martyrs* (1948), *L'Église des temps barbares* (1950). In three critical biographies, Daniel-Rops studied in particular the religious problem as it is reflected in the writings of *Rimbaud, Péguy,* and *Ernest Psichari.*

Henri Bremond is a historian of literature and religious thought in his monumental eleven-volume work *Histoire littéraire du sentiment religieux en France des guerres de religion à nos jours.* These volumes, appearing between 1916 and 1931, contain a considerable amount of literary criticism and judgment. The last volume brings the history to the end of the ancien régime.

In another work, of more modest proportions, Abbé Bremond shows himself hostile to the theories of Maurras and Daudet in a defense of romanticism: *Pour le romantisme.* He assigns to the romantics a role in literature that is comparable to the role of the mystics in the history of religion. This initial study of the poetic expression in its relationship to the religious experience, developed into a series of articles written in answer to critics who do not possess, according to Bremond, the "sense of mystery." These articles were published in book form in 1925: *La Poésie pure.* This was followed by *Prière et poésie* in which all the arts are studied as attempts on the part of artists, through the intermediaries of poetry, sound, color, to become a form of prayer.

Abbé Bremond looks upon scientific explanation of a work of art (any method resembling that of Taine, for example) as fundamentally impossible. The critic for Bremond remains the humanist, the man who first enjoys the beautiful and then teaches something about this enjoyment.

Bremond combined the temperament of an artist with the training and the attributes of a theologian. He came from the south, from Aix-en-Provence where he began his religious training, but lived for six years in England between the ages of seventeen and twenty-three, where he carried out the first part of his novitiat. In his major work, *Histoire littéraire du sentiment religieux en France*, Bremond studies the history or the drama of those who, in order to discover God, rely on themselves and on human reason. This he calls "anthropocentrism." Others, more privileged, are illuminated by a more direct contact with God. This way to the absolute, he designates as "theocentrism." Bossuet is the type of writer who approaches an understanding of God by purely human means. Fénelon is studied by Bremond and favored by him as the type of writer who uses divine means. During the decade after the First World War, *Histoire littéraire* was the one critical work that belonged to the tradition of Sainte-Beuve, that by its proportions recalled such a work as *Port-Royal*, and that combined the humanistic spirit with erudition.

Jacques Rivière began his literary career as a friend and almost a disciple of Gide and Proust. In 1909 he married Isabelle, the sister of Alain-Fournier, and became editor of *La Nouvelle revue française* which he directed until 1918. In his most personal book, of a religious nature, *A la trace de Dieu* (1925), he traces his spiritual itinerary as an intellectual who became a believer in order to understand the world and himself. He practiced his faith in a direct and almost childlike way. His importance today, his importance as a critic, is to be found, not so much in his essays *Études*, as in his correspondence with such figures as Claudel, Alain-Fournier, and Antonin Artaud.

When he was collecting his essays for *Études*, Rivière

seemed to be hesitating between the example of Gide and that of Claudel. He included studies of both writers, as well as an essay on Baudelaire, in the volume of 1912, and then announced his conversion in 1913. His critical writing does not reveal a specific method. His influence has been one of divination and prophecy. Very early in his career he advised the new writer to explore the subconscious and the activity of dreams: "Introduction à la métaphysique du rêve," published in one of the early issues of the *Nouvelle revue française.* He was instrumental in making this publication into much more than a magazine. It became the center of a new orientation in criticism in its reception of foreign literatures and in the importance given to problems of psychology, art, and philosophy. It laid the foundation of a new humanism in harmony with the discoveries and problems of the twentieth century by publishing some of the critical writings of Gide and Valéry, of Rivière and Paulhan, and Emmanuel Cioran, an essayist of Rumanian origin.

Jean Calvet was ordained a priest in 1896 and taught briefly in the Institut Catholique de Toulouse where he had been a seminarian. Most of his career was spent as dean and then rector at the Institut Catholique de Paris. Deeply admired by his students, Mgr. Calvet showed himself to be not only a critic and historian, but also a man endowed with considerable psychological penetration. He directed the publication of a long *Histoire de la littérature française,* and himself wrote the volume dealing with religious literature from François de Sales to Fénelon. His *Renouveau catholique dans la littérature contemporaine* (1927), was the first history of the movement often referred to as the Catholic Renascence in French letters.

The term "Christian existentialist" has been constantly used to describe the philosophical position of Gabriel Marcel, despite his disapproval. He received an *agrégation de philosophie* in 1910 and taught in various lycées in the provinces before he taught at the Sorbonne. He was baptized in the Catholic Church in 1929.

His works are mediations much more than systematic deductions of a philosophical system. His philosophy is existential and Christian in the sense that it is a search for his being, an effort to understand the ontological mystery. Marcel asks the questions of Pascal: Who am I? What am I without God? Freedom is like the air a man breathes: he has all of it he needs. Dogmas are the way to the absolute, and man is the viator.

This philosopher's principal theme is not freedom (as it is for Sartre) but participation. Sartre's philosophy of freedom has made any relationship with others very difficult. Gabriel Marcel seeks first a participation with being, with what he calls intersubjectivity. His freedom is first his relationship with the world and with history. He recognizes the painful ambiguity of man's fate, but he refuses to associate it with the absurd. He insists upon the value of the human person and on man's effort to surpass himself. His fame as a thinker has grown steadily since 1944, since the end of the war, with the advent of "committed literature" (*littérature engagée*) and the vogue of existentialism.

Emmanuel Mounier was far more engaged in action, throughout his career, than in speculative thinking. As a young man he was influenced by Péguy. In the late twenties he often attended the Sunday evening gatherings at the home of Jacques and Raïssa Maritain in Meudon, where he announced plans to found a new magazine for the propagation of his belief. *Esprit* appeared first in 1932. At Mounier's death in 1950, the direction of the magazine was taken over by Albert Béguin until his death in 1957.

Mounier called his own brand of philosophy "personalism" (*le personnalisme*). This doctrine concerning the human person is based upon a very sincere, very strongly motivated desire of Mounier to reestablish Christainity in its intellectual, moral, social, and political domains. He sees capitalism as a structure impeding the liberation of man and calls for a socialistic organization of production and consumption. The political and economic character of man occupies a large part of the editorials in *Esprit*.

Le personnalisme is not a system, in the sense of Sartrian existentialism, but it is an effort to unite materialism and idealism. Emmanuel Mounier's book, *Introduction aux existentialismes*, is a short, simple and illuminating exposé of the principal philosophical ideas of our day. In speaking of the insufficiency of reason, he refers especially to Pascal whom Mounier looks upon as the thinker opposing the rationalism of Descartes and those who study science at the expense of the life and the death of man. Mounier claims that almost every theme of twentieth-century existentialism is in Pascal: the opposition of custom and force to truth and justice; man's duplicity; the paradox of eternal truth and that of *un être existant*; the meeting of eternity and historicity, of the infinite and the finite, of hope and despair, of the ineffable and language. The theme of Tertullian, "I believe because it is absurd" (*credo quia absurdum*), is related to the theme of the "incomprehensible" in Pascal. Mounier defines "commitment" as an irruption, a bursting forth (*éclatement*), a release from man's subjectivism to an acceptance of his position (*situation*) in the world. Existental man cannot be indifferent to the finite world. Commitment is a rule for a sane existence.

5

Existentialism

Since 1940, philosophy seems to be everywhere in French literature, not only in technical philosophical treatises, but in novels, plays, essays, films. It is especially merged with literary criticism. Existentialist writers, in the wake of the surrealists, and postexistentialist writers of the 1950's and 1960's have asked questions and proposed answers concerning the nature of man, in order to define man in some manner that would befit the contemporary world and make up for the failure of science to quiet the metaphysical bewilderment of man. At no other time in the history of French literature has philosophy been so popular an adjunct to literature and so clearly directed and controlled literary criticism. The writings of Gabriel Marcel, Jean Wahl, and Merleau-Ponty are at times quite close to literary criticism. Sartre and Camus, whose names have been so often coupled since the liberation, are beyond any doubt two major literary critics whose methods of criticism and whose aesthetic judgments cannot be separated from their philosophical understanding of man.

During the last year of the forties, Sartre was the most discussed writer in France, and probably in Europe. He had become the acknowledged leader of existentialism, the predominant philosophical-literary movement of the entire decade of the forties. His novels, plays, and essays have now reached a wide international audience. But the center of his work is a dialectics on man, which is presented in its fullest and most technical form in *L'Être et le néant* (translated into English, *Being and Nothingness,*

by Hazel Barnes). The work is the basis for an understanding of the philosophical assumption of all the writings of Sartre and of existentialism in general.

Sartre's importance comes from the fact that his vision
of the world and of man corresponds to many of the
fundamental concepts in the modern consciousness.
L'Être et le néant deals almost exclusively with the subject
of ontology, with the interpretation of being. Philosophical considerations abound in Sartre's novels, plays, and
polemical writings. In *L'Être et le néant*, his account is
more detached and more objective. Sartre propounds that
human existence is its own value; it creates its own values.
It is not a means, as Christian philosophy is, of discovering transcendental values. The existentialist believes that
man is free, and that this total freedom, which at first is
inseparable from the experience of anguish, is the basis of
man's reconciliation with self. That is why Sartre calls
existentialism a humanism.

He describes anguish (*angoisse*) as the immediate
datum of freedom (*la véritable donnée immédiate de
notre liberté*). Man is anguish (*nous sommes angoisse*). If
we are anguish and try to escape it, we are providing an
example of bad faith (*mauvaise foi*). When we are aware
of making a choice for ourselves, we experience both
anguish and responsibility. "Nothingness" does not have a
bad connotation in Sartre's philosophy. It refers to a detachment of consciousness in its relationship to matter. In
his effort to reconcile philosophical realism (the primal
existence of matter) with philosophical idealism (the primal existence of consciousness), Sartre does not appear as
the traditional materialistic atheist. He is, in fact, fairly
scornful of science. His basic assumption is the belief that
since reality is accessible to man only through his consciousness, the sole study of the philosopher is man's
consciousness.

The chapters constituting the essay *Qu'est-ce que la
littérature?* first appeared as articles in *Les Temps modernes* and in book form in 1948. The writing of this essay
was an elaborate answer given by Sartre to the many

questions and attacks he had received concerning the precise meaning he applied to the word *engagement* (commitment). This critical-theoretical explanation of his position practically coincided with the founding of his magazine, *Les Temps modernes*, in 1945.

Early in the essay, Sartre indicates that he is not speaking of poetry, that he does not consider poetry a commitment. He has omitted from his analysis any poetic or metaphysical form of writing in favor of prose-writing which is destined to serve a moral and political action in society. He defines, in 1946, the moral mission of the writer as that of illuminating the historical period in which he lives and influencing it. As he develops his arguments, he draws quite ostensibly from the basic tenets of his philosophy. Man in himself is not a reality, he is a *project*. He is not free not to choose. He is committed. He has to take sides. The act of abstaining is itself a choice.

In referring to the past, to the position of the writer in past epochs, he seems to condemn the withdrawal which the intellectual and the artist and the contemplative once believed was their right and even their obligation. Sartre claims that the writer is involved in the problems and the disasters of his age. He is *dans le coup*. A piece of writing is a commitment, an enterprise by means of which the author embraces his age.

Sartre is hostile to many matters in the past history of literature. The seventeenth century, for example, in its studies of man's personality, did not take into consideration all the economic, political, and religious factors. If it had, such a method of investigation would have resembled Taine's famous theory of *race, milieu, et moment*. Yet Sartre manifests considerable scorn for Taine, to whom he owes perhaps more than he acknowledges or realizes. Throughout his career he has spoken almost begrudgingly of his very few literary admirations. He has been accused by his detractors of not liking literature, and even of undermining the aesthetic principles of literature. His open hostility to Flaubert is somewhat explained by Flaubert's indifference toward the Commune. Sartre *does* like the literary art; it would be unfair to affirm the contrary. But he does not believe literature is immortal, and he fears that literature is threatened by the very historical processes which today threaten the existence of mankind.

Persistent animosities he expresses help to eliminate some of his theories. He has little sympathy for Paul Valéry, for example, whose writings he finds too abstract. Proust he denounces for many "bourgeois" traits: Proust *le rentier*. Pascal's commitment, in his writing an apology of Christianity, would be looked upon as the wrong kind of commitment, that destined to preserve a value. In the Sartrian sense, a commitment should help to bring about a change and initiate an evolution. With the philosopher's marked emphasis on the present and the future, he will inevitably tend to minimize literature of the past. He believes in the instability of human nature and the instability of so-called literary masterpieces.

Writers are men no different from the rest of mankind. By the mere fact that they are writers, they do not rise above other men or live separated from history. They are involved in history, as everyone else is. If they are faithful to their vocation, their writings will be an irritant for their age. Sartre often insists that literature should not bring comfort to readers, but on the contrary it should raise disturbing questions and initiate anxiety in the hearts of readers. One of the functions of a writer is to harass society by inducing feelings of guilt.

Sartre underscores the social responsibility of the writer. He tests each writer with the same kind of question: What have you done for the people of your country? What have you done for all of mankind? Disparagingly he speaks of academic culture, of a fruitless kind of study carried on in libraries, those isolated places he compares to tombs. He deprecates that sense of social indifference and irresponsibility arising from a certain kind of study and bookish research. This attitude of submission to the past would contradict the existentialist assumption that man has to be perpetually redefined.

Sartre never loses sight of what appears to him and to many other thinkers as the crisis in modern thought. One of the ways by which this crisis may be averted are repaired would be to restore to literature its full social function. This means that the writer must write for his age at the expense of any preoccupation with the history of the past or with the theology of eternity. The writer is in a "situation." This word, used by Sartre as the title of the volume which included the essay *Qu'est-ce que la littérature?* (*Situations II*), has a specific technical meaning. The *situation* is the synthesis of all the forces that form and develop the individual. The writer's age is looked upon as an absolute, a living absolute, and Sartre is particularly harsh on a Christian literature that would stress the immortality of the soul and any relationship between the living and the dead.

The eloquence of Sartre is apparent when he analyzes the writer's duty as that of searching for truth concerning temporal causes and then giving expression to this truth, even if such a gesture means for the writer that he is speaking in opposition to the majority. Sartre would believe that in working for the exoneration and rehabilitation of Calas, Voltaire grew in stature as a man and writer; in signing the document *J'accuse!*, Émile Zola fulfilled his function of writer; by writing such a book as *Voyage au Congo*, André Gide reached the truth of his vocation. These three examples of major French writers in three different centuries, who, by espousing a cause of their day, were committed, in the existentialist sense, were judicious choices for Sartre. However, it can be questioned whether their action in the cause would have had any effect if they had not previously established their literary reputation by the writing of other kinds of books.

What Is Literature? is a manifesto and the most lucid commentary we have on the early books of Sartre. After providing first in *La Nausée* and *Huis clos* a picture of the egoism and pharisaism of contemporary society, Sartre then offered this text of theory in which he tries to prove how impossible it should be for the modern writer to avoid participating in the problems of his age.

Behind Sartre's advocated position for the contemporary writer, namely that of assuming the risks for the cause of everyone, is a series of positions characteristic of successive epochs. In the Middle Ages the writer was the *clerc*, a man essentially engaged in the service of God. In the Classical Age the writer was a member of a cultivated society, a man eager to establish a bond of equality between himself and his public. In the eighteenth century, the age of the "philosophers," the writer became the militant fighting for the rights of man. But since that time, he tends to be the parasite, dependent upon the favors of wealth, and to delude himself with specious theories, such as "art for art's sake." In a peremptory fashion, Sartre demolishes the more indulgent, the more generous theories concerning the artist in our world.

It was possible at one time, in the forties, to look upon Jean-Paul Sartre as a master surrounded by disciples. He no longer has this position, but many writers and thinkers agree with Sartre on the necessity today for a "committed literature." This central and very serious concept of responsibility, apparent on many pages in Sartre's manifesto, is not unique to his thought in the twentieth century. It is a persistent theme in the work of such French writers as Péguy, Bernanos, and Malraux. Such writers would agree with Sartre that our ways of living and the accomplishments of our life depend solely upon us. There is no ready-made doctrine or facile system which will guide our life, without the play of our own will, without the force of our own responsibility.

The total effect of Sartre's writings (and this is fully apparent in *What Is Literature?*) is condemnatory. His is one of the harshest condemnations of today's society.

And yet throughout his relentless criticism of the conditions of human activity today, Sartre is seeking and proposing a new set of values. In one form or another, he is constantly asking whether the writer in our day will allow, in some mute passivity, the catastrophe of another war. His essay on literature proposes an aesthetics based upon the notion of commitment. This commitment applies to prose writers whose art is essentially an art of meaning. If prose is the art of meaning, then, as Sartre argues, he cannot conceive of art as not being "engaged." Many of the points he makes turn his treatise into something that resembles a psychoanalytical history of contemporary history. Other considerations give it the form of a political guidebook for the writer's use. But throughout the work one follows a closely reasoned argument of Sartre's fundamental position: man's responsibility, and his anxiety that accompanies this responsibility.

On several counts Sartre's name has been associated with Voltaire: not only in the large number of books he has published and in their variety, but also in the writer's hatred of hypocrisy and in his conviction that literature is an integral part of life. The two men resemble one another in their active minds, the extensiveness of their knowledge, their power of polemicists, the continuous and impassioned rapport each established with his time. Sartre demonstrates a greater range in the tone of his affirmations, in the absolutism of his opinions, in the fear he expresses for the future fate of literature. He has systematized his thought far more rigorously than Voltaire, and has remained faithful to a given political terminology, that of dialectical materialism. The stories of *Candide* and *Micromégas* illustrate and defend the philosophy of Voltaire, as the pages of Sartre's essay illumine *Les Mains sales* and *Les Séquestrés d'Altona*.

In *Qu'est-ce que la littérature?* Sartre never deviates for long from the proposed subject of his essay, and he very skillfully fuses much of his philosophy with this discussion of aesthetics. If there is any such concept as an absolute, it must be there, he argues, where history is unfolding, where history is being lived—in the present. He gives to the word "reconciliation" an immediate and significant use, when he advocates in his essay a reconciliation between author and reader. Such a change will then bring about what he hopes for, what he calls for: the writer's assumption of his age in order to change his age.

In his short study of Baudelaire, Sartre has written an existentialist psychoanalysis. The poet is studied as the

case history of a man who refused to choose his life in the
existentialist sense. The existentialist has to create his own
meaning out of life, he has to renew his life and assume it
at each instant. But most men (Baudelaire is a leading
example for Sartre) avoid this continuous effort. Baudelaire claimed he was, like his hero Poe, a *maudit*, an
outcast, the suffering artist unable to change his fate,
unable to escape his bad luck (*guignon*). Sartre would say,
and does say in his essay, that Baudelaire, early in life,
made himself into a definitive statuelike, petrified being in
order to escape all responsibility. Sartre the critic describes
Baudelaire as a man leaning down (*un homme penché*),
looking at himself, looking at his past. He made his enemies, Aupick his father-in-law and Jeanne Duval his mistress, into his judges. Before Sartre's book on Baudelaire,
the poet's life had been interpreted by his biographers as a
failure in the human sense. Sartre interprets this failure as
a carefully cultivated, a willed failure. Baudelaire had, for
Sartre, the life he deserved.

By accepting passively the harsh judgments made
against him, Baudelaire abdicated before life and expressed a persistent fear of choosing. Whenever he was
accused, he pleaded guilty. Sartre insists on his conviction
that Baudelaire did not want friends in his life, but rather
he wanted judges in order to indulge his masochistic tendencies.

In his study, Sartre is not concerned with the poetry of
Baudelaire, but with the man himself in his life. At several
points in his discussion he leaves the objective, the neutral
ground of analysis, and speaks as accuser. In particular, he
deflates the importance of Baudelaire's personal journal
(*Fusées* and *Mon coeur mis à nu*) which by other critics
has been looked upon as equalling the *Pensées* of Pascal!

When Sartre's long study of Jean Genet was published
in 1952, it appeared immediately as one of his most unusual books, and one of his most significant. The volume is
a preface, of six hundred pages, a philosophical preface on
the profligacy of Genet's life and on the importance of
Genet's worth. *Saint Genet, comédien et martyr* appeared

at the peak of Sartre's fame, at a moment when his influence was predominent in France.

Sartre's study is valuable on many counts: for the revelation it provides on Genet's art, for its minute critical examination of Genet's novels (only a few of the pages are devoted to the first two plays), for the philosophical reflections concerning the problem of evil, for the brilliant way in which Genet's case is used to illustrate existentialism.

Genet had boasted that his work is the apology of evil, and Sartre devotes considerable time in an effort to prove that evil is a kind of myth created by the respectable people of a civilization. The rules of the good life are such that those who do evil are used by the respectable as scapegoats. The wicked commit the deeds the respectable do not dare to commit. This theory would seem to have some connection with Genet's childhood and adolescence, spent largely in reformatory schools and prisons, where an early knowledge and practice of evil were almost inevitable.

In *Saint Genet,* as well as in every other book by Sartre, the value of man is described as having its basis in the concept of freedom. Through the power of his freedom, man contracts an obligation to life. Genet's existence, even in its scandalous aspect, illustrates for Sartre the freedom that the respectable members of society will never know. They are in fact protected from this knowledge by their law courts that condemned and imprisoned Jean Genet.

Sartre's central thesis on Genet is not easy to condense and restate. In any attempt to understand a given human life, Sartre would claim that there are serious limitations in a purely psychoanalytical interpretation, as well as in a purely Marxist interpretation. For the philosopher, the measure of such an understanding lies in a man's concept of freedom, in the way in which a man's freeedom comes to grips with his fate. A man's existence is first controlled and crushed by all the determining factors, by all the fates that play on it. Sartre considers the literary work of Genet the projection, the imaginary picture of his life. His literary genius is identical with his determination (i.e., the exercise of his freedom) to live the drama of his own nature, up to the very ultimate consequence of this drama.

Sartre's study is a generous and a fascinating gloss on Genet's experience which, no matter how deprived it was of the natural comforts and assurances, has been realized through the power of words, by means of the literary art. At every step of the way, Genet has known what he was doing—hence Sartre's term to designate him, *comédien* or actor. And Genet never failed to acknowledge the condition imposed upon him by society when he was young— hence, the second term in the title of *martyr*. (It should perhaps be added that Sartre's title is suggested by the title of Rotrou's play of the seventeenth century, *Saint Genet*.)

Volume I of *Situations* appeared in 1947 and is a collection of articles that had been published in various periodicals between 1939 and 1945. It includes studies of Faulkner, Dos Passos, Mauriac, Giraudoux, Ponge, and one of the earliest critical pieces on Camus, "Explication de *L'Étranger*."

After analyzing the historical importance of *L'Étranger* and the philosophical dilemma the novel raises, Sartre then refers to the Camus essay, *Le Mythe de Sisyphe*, which appeared a few months after *L'Étranger*, and discusses the theme of the absurd. Then he returns to *L'Étranger* in order to explain it in terms of the concept of the absurd.

A strong friendship between Sartre and Albert Camus began at the time of the resistance movement during the war, and lasted approximately ten years. In his essay on *L'Étranger*, Sartre shows a marked sympathy for Camus and considerable agreement with his thought. When, in later years, differences did arise between them, Sartre recalled the moment of mutual understanding and admiration. Sartre had admired Meurseault, hero of *L'Étranger*, whose honesty forced him to refuse to say he loved his mother. Sartre had admired Camus for reflecting the conflicts of the period, for manifesting a belief in life, for defending social causes, for his love for beauty.

Sartre and Camus had always indicated philosophical differences, but they had the same public in France. Their natures were different: Camus, more the poet, had great purity in his writing; and Sartre, more the critic, had greater richness and animation of ideas. They represented a striking opposition, and the history of French letters has always favored this type of opposition. Camus names as absurd the divorce between the impulse of man toward the eternal and the finite character of nature and human nature. This concept is foreign to the thought of Sartre whose "nausea" has little to do with the impulse of Camus toward a communion with the beauty of nature.

Camus's book of 1951, *L'Homme révolté*, was not liked by Sartre, and one of Sartre's fellow workers in *Les Temps modernes*, Francis Jeanson, wrote a bitter attack on it. The estrangement between Camus and Sartre was consummated when Sartre pointed out his belief that *L'Homme révolté* testified to a philosophical incompetence and that it was composed of bits of knowledge hastily put together.

Albert Camus always insisted that he was not an existentialist in a literal sense. However, it is impossible not to associate him with the doctrine because of his sharp awareness of the absurdity of the world. This sense of absurdity did not lead Camus to a philosophical pessimism. His philosophical attitudes are clearly stated in his essay *Le Mythe de Sisyphe* (1943) and in his two novels, *L'Étranger* (1942) and *La Peste* (1947).

A Christian existentialist will look upon existence as the individual in his relationship with transcendence. He will say that existentialism is basically religious. Camus secularizes theological themes. He defines, for example, the absurd in *Le Mythe de Sisyphe* as sin without the concept of God—*l'absurde, c'est le péché sans Dieu*.

The world is not reasonable for Camus, and man is an outsider (*étranger*). The man who feels absurd is simply the man who accepts the evidence. No notion of sin is comprehensible to him. Faced with the choice between history and eternity, Camus stated that he chose history. *Entre l'histoire et l'éternel, j'ai choisi l'histoire parce que j'aime les certitudes.* Camus welcomes the emotions that come to a man who struggles. He believes in the metaphysical value of human solidarity. In choosing the human order, he believes he is negating the sacred, or the order of Christianity, which he has defined as a philosophy of injustice.

Camus is the witness of man without God. He is the philosopher of the absurd. And yet he transcends the absurd as he embraces the human cause by means of the dual experience of revolt and solidarity. The movement of revolt is a positive act by which man becomes aware of a truth that is greater than the truth of any individual destiny.

At the beginning of his career, Camus gave in *Le Mythe de Sisyphe* the picture of a hero absurd in his passion and in his torment. He is a worker in hell whose labor is useless. But he is a man conscious of what he is doing, aware of its absurdity. The experience of a gigantic effort against great odds fills his heart. Camus says that we must imagine Sisyphus as happy. As he rolls his rock up the hill in hell, it is imperative that we try, with all our will, to live in a universe that is meaningless.

After the publication of *L'Étranger* Albert Camus's work became an effort to reconcile his faith in life with his sense of the absurdity of life. The articles in *Combat*, written during the months immediately following the liberation, offered as much hope to the French at that time as the example of the action of General de Gaulle. This was perhaps the moment of Camus's greatest moral influence. He was the frank, outspoken defender of human values. He never denied the repugnance he felt for the world in which he lived, but likewise he never ceased claiming a solidarity with men who suffer in that world.

For Camus, the writer has to serve both the suffering of man and the cause of beauty. He measures the greatness of the artist by the equilibrium he maintains in this dual vocation, and in this regard cites the names of Molière and Melville in his essay, *Que peut faire l'artiste dans le monde d'aujourd'hui?*

At the time of Camus's death in January 1960, an automobile accident on Route Nationale 5, he had become much more than a writer in France. He was much more than the author of *La Peste* and *La Chute* for those Frenchmen who may have felt a national pride in his receiving the Nobel Prize two years earlier, at the age of forty-four. He occupied a privileged place, with only two other living writers, Sartre and Malraux, that of leader and inspirer for the younger intellectuals.

A large number of Frenchmen had learned to think with Camus, to derive hope and sustenance from his books. He had become a moralist, one of those French writers who stress the purely human values of conduct and who occupy the highest and most original place in French letters. This very position of moralist in the case of Camus was looked upon by Sartre as a defect or as a failure to meet the greater challenge to participate actively in the political events of the moment. The position of moralist is far too prudent for Sartre, the *engagé*.

Camus's birth in poverty in Algeria, his revolt against the condition of man and his role of *résistant*, his glory and apotheosis as a writer, his accidental death seem today the elements of a legend. Death was for Albert Camus the consecration of his inconsistencies. The reasonableness of his mind was always being baffled by the rapture of his senses and by the dismay he felt on examining the universe. The country boy and the philosopher remained simultaneously present in him. He spoke of the two possible ways of living in our day—by solitude and by solidarity—and he advocated neither one. Sartre once called him one of the gifted heirs of Chateaubriand, and in that definition evoked the curious amalgam of traits that he demonstrated: the exotic, the idealistic, the quasi-Christian.

In 1952, Maurice Merleau-Ponty was given the chair of philosophy in the Collège de France. He had joined, in 1945, the group of men and women who founded *Les Temps modernes*. This magazine, directed by Sartre, was from the beginning the official existential periodical.

In his philosophy, Merleau-Ponty avoids the two extremes: a total dependence on reason, and a total exclusion of reason. He does not refuse what defines man as an *existant*: the world, the body of man, and the consciousness of man. In the introduction to his important book *Phénoménologie de la perception* (1945), he speaks of the philosopher's return to things (*revenir aux choses mêmes*) and says it is a return to the world before our knowledge of the world. This would be comparable to our experience of a forest, a field, or a river before our knowledge of geography. Before a man philosophizes, he establishes a fundamental contract with the world. The analysis concerning the phenomenal body of man and its opening out to others in the world reveal a structure which Merleau-Ponty calls a *présence*, a temporal presence attached to other people in the world.

Philosophy is not a series of concepts for Merleau-Ponty, and neither is it a body of knowledge. It is rather an awareness, a spirit of vigilance characterized by a refusal to accept ready-made truth and by an interest in continuous reflections. Such a philosophy cannot avoid reflecting on contemporary history and participating in it. The philosopher is committed to others and not solely to himself and to truth as he sees it. There are very few anarchists among philosophers, says Merleau-Ponty. It is quite possible for a philosopher to be both detached as a thinker and enrolled in the service of man.

After receiving the *agrégation de philosophie*, Simone de Beauvoir taught philosophy in Marseille, Rouen, and Paris. She joined the editorial board of *Les Temps modernes* in 1945. Her meeting with Sartre changed her life and transformed a carefully brought up, traditionally educated young lady into an almost legendary figure of Saint-

Germain-des-Prés. Her novel, *L'Invitée* (1943), is a declaration of love for life, a vibrant feeling for existence, a kind of answer to Sartre's *La Nausée*. It was the beginning of an imposing series of books: four novels, two books of travel, a play, four essays, two large volumes of *Le Deuxième sexe*, and three volumes of autobiography. *Les Mandarins* (1954), won the Goncourt Prize and revealed to a wide public an analysis of left-wing political problems.

Mme de Beauvoir has recorded that at the age of twenty, she felt outside of life. Then a change took place and she began participating in the world, in political combat. She has used some of her writing to express her opinion on crucial issues. She looks upon the essay as an exposé of ideas, as a text used to provoke her readers. In the novel, she attempts to show life in its ambiguities but draws no philosophical or moral conclusions.

In the third volume of her autobiography, *La Force des choses*, she records the ultimate consequences of her life with Jean-Paul Sartre and her friendship with other writers. She analyzes many problems in those years of French history (1944–1962), when Sartre, and the group of writers associated with him, took over a moral and literary leadership under the aegis of existentialism. Mme de Beauvoir is decidedly anti-Gaullist, and she does not hesitate to name the Fifth Republic a Fascist régime. Albert Camus, in his disagreement with existentialism and in his attitude toward the Algerian crisis, comes off as badly as Charles de Gaulle in *La Force des choses*. Sectarian and resentful, especially when she attacks religion, she elucidates the views of an existentialist thinker when she rejects certain traditions and laws of society.

Much of the best critical writing on existentialism has been done by American and English critics. Before 1950 they tended to interpret the philosophy as one of decadence and moral corruption, as one of intense pessimism resulting from the war. This view has now been reversed in the studies of William Barrett, James Collins, and Iris

Murdoch. The French critics, in the warm reception they gave in 1964 to *Les Mots*, seemed eager to look upon Sartre again as an artist. He had probably exaggerated his doctrine of commitment in the earlier years, in his desire to see the man of letters assume the role of conscience director. The passionate and even sentimental side of Sartre's nature has not yet been fully explored by the critics. *Les Mots*, his autobiography of childhood, is as fine a work as he has ever composed. In his aspiration to universal values, evident in his earliest writings when he spoke of his sense of responsibility for all his fellowmen, Sartre takes his place in the tradition of the French *moralistes*.

6

At Midcentury
Introduction to the New Criticism

André Malraux, in his studies on the psychology of art, collected in the volume V*oix du silence* (1951), refers to the arts of all ages and all worlds. The prehistoric cave drawings coexist with Braque and Picasso. His work is really on the subject of human genius, on an extraordinary awareness of man and his destiny. He insists on convincing the reader that an artistic creation is the justification of the mystery of our life. Because of the vigor and the perceptiveness of this hymn to art, Malraux was chosen by many younger minds in the 1950's as a critic and spiritual guide. His eloquence is always the most vibrant in the passages dealing with the relationship between man and the sacred. One thought above all others he never tires of reiterating, namely that art does not imitate life, but that it imitates art and reveals life. The great apology he makes for art is its immortality, at least the breath of immortality that permeates it.

Such subjects as the resistance movement and the concentration-camp world did not in any way create a literary school. In fact, twentieth-century literature, despite the significant programs of surrealism in the 1930's and existentialism in the 1940's, is characterized by an absence of strongly organized and formulated literary movements. Nothing today is comparable to the romantic or the symbolist schools of the nineteenth century. Twentieth-century literature in France may well be as rich as that of the nineteenth century, but it is far more confused and anarchical. In its search for an order of intellectual and formal values, contemporary literature has grown into an art of critical assessment. The four masters who have dominated the half century—Proust, Valéry, Gide, and Claudel; André Breton and surrealists in general; Jean-Paul Sartre and existentialists in general; François Mauriac and other Catholic writers—have all devoted large portions of their work to critical statement, to a serious effort to explain and justify the more purely creative part of their writing.

W. H. Auden once characterized our age as one of anxiety. To literary observers it would seem to be an age of criticism. To no specific culture is the phrase more applicable than to that of France. The current literary fashions of Paris are meticulously examined, evaluated, and reexamined not only by the French themselves, who have a natural proclivity for criticism, but by literature students and scholars in every country. At this moment in the history of French letters pure creativity in the realms of fiction and verse, for example, seem to have diminished, and the activity of the critic has developed with such boldness and brilliance that it has taken over first place. In the immediate history of letters, it began with Sartre with the critical position of existentialism at the close of the war. His key text *Qu'est-ce que la littérature?* is still being pondered and still being answered; but long before Sartre, at the beginning of the century, it was strong in Péguy, and it continued to be strong in writers known primarily for other genres: in Cocteau, in his intermittent flashes of critical insights; in Mauriac, in his analyses of the novelist's art; in Montherlant, in the prefaces to his plays.

The French public enjoys the entertainment of critical debate as much as it enjoys the first performances of a new play or the first reading of a new novel. Critical debate starts up quickly in France, and soon the new work itself (or the old work), which initiated the debate, is lost sight of, and the abstractions begin to mount, the formulations of a new system and a new creed are disseminated. It is not long before the entire cause of literature is refined or even demolished, and something resembling the "quarrel between the ancients and the moderns" is evolved, or a vast body of writing appears, almost overnight, as complex as the assembled theories on the origins of the *chansons de geste*. Nothing is spared in these quarrels: private lives, religious belief, patriotism. Everything can be used against and for, because there is a chance that one of the debates will become a vital chapter in the history of French literature. This would seem to be the case in the theories of literary criticism as they have developed in the course of the sixties, and in their origins discernible now in the other decades of the century.

When the present generation of practicing critics, in France and in this country, were students of literature in the universities and writing their first articles and first books, Baudelaire, for example, was looked upon as the initiator of symbolism, and the most serious, the most gifted founder of the new type of art. But today, in the late sixties, symbolism seems to them more a completed historical movement, the achieved development and goal of romanticism. Baudelaire is therefore more a classical writer than a revolutionist. The same can be said of the critical fate of Flaubert, once looked upon as the founder of the modern novel and today considered (except by Mme Sarraute) a writer who belongs almost completely to the past, to an era and an ideal that have come to an end and who has therefore entered upon that rather stark domain we call history.

At its simplest and most unpretentious level, literary criticism aims at informing the reader concerning the book in question, and then elucidating difficulties and obscurities that may be in the book or in the writer. On a slightly higher level, the critic, if he is favorably disposed toward the book, will attempt to stimulate interest in it, to account for the stimulation he felt on reading the book, to communicate something of the pleasure he derived from it, and to analyze the reasons for this pleasure. Beyond the goals, which are useful and admirable in themselves, is the conviction, to be reaffirmed by the critics and substantiated by them, that literature is the revealer of man's consciousness at its highest level of self-knowledge and self-awareness. Literature is the communication to the reader of the writer's experience of his imagination. In order to analyze and judge this communication, the critic has to compare it with other communications.

With the new French critics, such as Georges Poulet, Gaston Bachelard, Roland Barthes, Jean-Pierre Richard, and Lucien Goldmann, this comparison and this judgment tend to be expressed in terms of a system, in terms of an ideological position, which allows the critic to be vigorous, forceful, and lucid, but which also tends to make him overrigid, overdictatorial. A host of younger critics, often students or disciples of the older critics, have become so absorbed in dissecting technical devices in literary genres, that the newest of the new critics in France have neglected or not dared to face the great myths in the literature of the midcentury and the post midcentury.

Traditionally criticism is an explanation of the experience of reading. It does not add obscurity to the work criticized, but allows for an understanding of the pleasure or displeasure felt in the experience of reading.

But today criticism has become something quite different from this kind of explanation and judgment. It has become a source of knowledge concerning man. The difficulty of the new criticism and its intricate subtlety are its characteristic traits. There is a far greater difference between Sainte-Beuve and Maurice Blanchot than between such poets as Rimbaud and René Char.

It might seem that the richness and variety of contemporary French criticism exist because of the penury of new creative works. A more sound explanation is probably to be found in the development and expansive growth of the human sciences: psychoanalysis in particular, psychology, phenomenology, anthropology, and sociology. The literary critic of the nineteenth century had only a rudimentary knowledge of what today is called sociology and psychology. Much of today's criticism is an application of anthropological studies based upon extensive research.

The new criticism is actually a new attitude toward language, looked upon as a great force in man. Language has come to be looked upon as the definition of man. Criticism is now a morality in the sense that it is that force in man which allows him to understand himself and other men. And, if it is so considered a force in man, it is also a force in civilization. It is primarily a force joining one man with another man: namely, a reader with a writer. The critic is the writer who joins the literature of one nation with the literature of another. A critic is an intercessor between men of his own country and between men of several countries. The concept of universal literature has today replaced the concept of a national literature, thanks to the critic.

The critic never forgets that he would have nothing to say if it were not for the creative writer, for the novelist, the poet, and the dramatist. And he never forgets that it is because of him and thanks to his critical mind that the work says what it has to say.

Even if the new critic tends to deprecate the biographical approach to a work of art, he does, inadvertently, and at times quite deliberately, explain literature through life when he speaks in Marxist or psychoanalytical terms. But the new criticism represents predominantly a return to the text, even the work of the Marxist Barthes and the psychoanalyst Bachelard. It is a new version of a traditional *explication de texte*, an explication of a text in its own terms. It is what might be called an immanent interpretation. Even if it does not always succeed, it attempts to avoid reducing a literary text to something extraliterary. It wills to be a narrowly circumscribed discipline.

Within the memory of those critics who are writing today is the typical university course where, rather than teaching the text inscribed on the program, *Tartuffe*, for example, the professor would devote his discoveries to the history of comedy before Molière, the biography of Molière up to the year when he wrote *Tartuffe*, and a review of Molière's comedies before *Tartuffe*.

In reaction to this extreme form of presenting a literary

text by avoiding it, the new school of criticism has been determined to look into the work from the beginning and to discuss it. Its goal is to follow the ways in the text itself that a literary sensitivity expresses itself and transmits its experience and vision. The language of the poet, the printed words on the page, is all that the critic needs for his appraisal.

A passive reading of *Madame Bovary*, for example, would make it appear as a series of events, characterized by banality, and masterfully drawn. A more active kind of reading, such as that advocated by the new critic, would reveal that the events narrated in the novel are reflected in the stagnating conscience of Emma Bovary who is practically immobilized. In Jean Rousset's essay on *Madame Bovary* (in *Forme et signification*), we see that the famous ball at the beginning of Emma's social career is simply a picture revolving in the eyes and heart of a woman already destroyed. The best pages of the new criticism give us the experience of a discovery: The internal architecture of a work suddenly comes into focus for the first time.

This is the form of textual analysis of which Charles Du Bos was the instigator. Other critics who best illustrate the method, between Du Bos in the 1930's, and Rousset's *Forme et signification* (1962), are Marcel Raymond (Rousset's teacher), Georges Poulet, Jean Starobinski, Jean-Pierre Richard, Georges Blin, Gaëtan Picon, and Maurice Blanchot. Another group of critics, in whose writing psychoanalytical analysis is more predominant, has been guided by the example of Gaston Bachelard, Albert Béguin, Charles Mauron, and Georges Bataille. These are not groups strictly separated by theory and practice. Several of the names could appear in both, Raymond and Blin, for example.

With the goal of criticism clearly announced as the analysis of "structures," the cleavage from the historical approach is obvious. By studying the internal biology of a work, its organization, its architecture, its phenomenology, the critic hopes to reach its real meaning and to understand the role of the reader as it was defined or implicated in the writer's intentions. Basically, this method is similar to the classical *explication de texte*, utilized so widely in secondary school education in France, and similar to the "new criticism" in America of the 1930's. In abandoning the analysis of all the circumstances that surround a given text, all the historical, geographical, and literary sources working on a text directly or indirectly, some of the new French critics have engaged upon such a subtle internal interpretation that it sometimes appears overdrawn and overpedantic. Every method of literary criticism has its dangers of heaviness of vocabulary and apparatus, as well as its pretentions of being unique and of being the sole discoverer of truth.

Those critics who demonstrate a sympathy for a Marxian philosophy of history form a third group, but here the alliances with the other two groups are so strong that there is often little need to consider them apart: Roland Barthes and Lucien Goldmann, for example.

The work of each of these new critics who have been publishing during the past fifteen or twenty years is distinctive. Each has his own style, his own obsessions and emphases. What unites them is a belief that criticism is literature about literature. Despite their many differences of temperament and style, when grouped together these critics do represent a new intellectual climate in France, a new and vigorous approach to an understanding of a work of art.

Their interest lies first and foremost in the literary work itself, in the book or the poem, and they avert their attention rigorously and deliberately from the writer himself. Respect for the text and a determination to understand it come first. This approach involves extensive quotation of the text and extensive commentary on the text.

The obvious intentions of a text, the surface meanings, are not those which hold the critic. He is interested in discovering and studying those intentions which are not immediately perceptible and which were not necessarily known by the author himself. The existence in a literary text of an unconscious intention is justified by modern psychological research. The latest meanings of a text seem as significant, if not more significant, than consciously formulated meanings.

In this search for the profounder meanings of a text, the critics have drawn extensively on traditional psychoanalysis as it is presented in the work of Freud and Jung. This is largely symbolic. The symbols are known in advance. For the most part, they have been already carefully named and classified. When the critic discovers them in a text, he does not have to understand them, but merely to explain them. Charles Mauron's studies of Mallarmé and Racine, and Sartre's studies of Baudelaire and Genet are brilliant examples of psychoanalytical criticism, in which every detail in a text can be examined as a sign or as a symptom.

Closely related to Sartrian psychoanalysis is Gaston Bachelard's method of analyzing a writer's imagination as it is expressed in his metaphors. Bachelard's work, which antedated Sartre's, represented something of a revolution in criticism. He sought to discover and study in the recurring metaphors of a writer the mythic significance, the archetypal dream which he believes characterizes and explains a poet's imagination. These archetypal patterns are seen to be related to the four elements: earth, water, fire, air. Bachelard's criticism is a psychoanalysis of matter. The substance (*la matière*) evoked by a poet corresponds to a state of feeling, to a mental state which accounts for the poem or the novel.

Whereas Mauron and Bachelard sought to follow in the writers they studied traces of the unconscious, Maurice Blanchot and Georges Poulet have demonstrated in their criticism greater attentiveness to those fully conscious traits in a work which mark a man or a writer and which illuminate his intentions and his accomplishments. In his analysis of several passages of an author Poulet establishes a set of observations, almost a dialectic, on the functioning of his consciousness, which goes beyond what a single text might reveal. Blanchot and Poulet do not study the symbols of an author as much as they study the recurring forms or structures of his mind and his writing.

The term "structuralism" as applied to literary criticism

has been used to group together such different critics as Poulet and Barthes, and the social anthropologist Lévi-Strauss. The basic assumption of this method is the belief that no single element of a work can be understood unless it is seen in its relationship with the entire work, and indeed with all the works of a given author. The sense of any detail must be referred to the sense of the whole. The perfect explication would be the ability to hear the resonance of an entire work in every sentence. The structuralist method is therefore a combination of analysis and synthesis, a study in which a detail is seen in a vast perspective, a treatise on the opposing movements of regression and progression.

A literary creation becomes for such a critic a network of obsessions, no one of which can be separated from the others. In a literary work human experiences, which had once been looked upon as distinct one from the other, are approached by the critic as forming a coherent whole, as representing correlations. Mallarmé's attraction to blue, to l'azur, is not one isolated obsession. It helps to explain and illuminate every other theme and the entire work of the poet.

The criteria used in this type of criticism are subjective. It is not a question of counting themes in a work and ascertaining the frequency of these themes. It is the discovering of areas or passages in the work where its profoundest significance is concentrated. This discovery is made thanks to the critic's sensitivity, to his sympathy for the author, to his flair for those personal and often concealed meanings of the author. It is often based on the critic's intuition concerning the position of a theme in a text, or its surroundings, or the elements it affects. Structuralist criticism is based upon a very private reading of the critic. If at the end of his study, the critic reaches objective illuminations concerning the text he is working on, the method by which he reaches them is a constant meditation on his own reactions, on his own feelings for a text. The personality of the critic is as much exposed as the sense of the text.

The goal of this new criticism may be quite complex. It may be more than merely the explication of a sonnet or even of a novel. It may be the understanding of the entire experience of an author in the light of all of his writings. It may even go beyond this, in order to illuminate the entire age in which the writer lived. Blanchot's study of Lautréamont, Barthes' study of Michelet, Sartre's long analysis of Genet, Goldmann's Racine, Richard's Mallarmé—these are a few, but eminently noteworthy, of new critical studies in which the aims of the critic are multiple. They are studies in which the structure of a work is related to the structure of a human experience and the structure of a society.

The position of the new critic is one of exceptional vigilance where he waits patiently, almost like a hunter, for the appearance of some original relationship between the writer and the world, a relationship that existed before the work was written and that orientated the work. The phenomenologists tell us that consciousness is at the basis of art, and it has to be consciousness of something. When Poulet uses such a phrase as *distance intérieure,* he means that distance between the self and the deepest form of consciousness that explains a man's actions in time and space. In one way or another, all of the new critics are explorers of signs and silence, of dreams and obsessions that existed at the birth of a literary work. They are also intent upon discovering the goal of a work, since every work is for them a "project." All the elements of a work's architecture exist in terms of a culmination.

Since the goal of a work is the transcription of the most secret part of the writer's ontology, the goal of the critic is the discovery of the secret motivation of the writer's being. It is the search for the self through the most secretive part of the work. The method by which this search is carried on is often borrowed from sciences and disciplines such as phenomenology, psychology, psychoanalysis, linguistics, semantics, and anthropology.

These men have helped to make of criticism an important cultural phenomenon. The dominant question in all their writing is: How is literature to be understood? They believed a form of criticism is being evolved, quite comparable in its newness to the new mathematics that is already being taught in our schools. Some of their writing has taken on the aspect of polemics in their opposition to the more traditional type of criticism that involved such subjects as biography, genres, literary generations, and the evolution of literary techniques. On both sides the controversy has been exaggerated until a neutral observer might easily believe that all critics are divided into two groups: those interested in writers and everything that surrounds a work; and those who are interested in the work of a writer and specifically in one text. The first type of critic would be classified by his absorption in literary history, in the historical value of a text; and the second, by his absorption in the work itself, in the aesthetic value of the work.

But such a clear dichotomy is not the case. The difference lies rather in the primacy of critical problems and the emphasis on ways of analyzing the problems. Traditionally, with Sainte-Beuve in the nineteenth century and Lanson in the twentieth, criticism starts with the writer as a man, in a study of his biography, his reading, and the influences operating on his life. The new critic tends to start with the work itself, to penetrate its meaning, and then, to explain the man by his work. The meanings of a text are not always those visible on its surface. On the opening pages of *L'Être et le néant*, Sartre distinguishes between *le conscient*, the consciousness of a man, and *le connu*, what a man knows about himself. *Le conscient* accompanies our psychological reactions, our behavior: in love, for example, and in our moral acts. *Le connu* presupposes an understanding of our conscious states, a certain degree of detachment from the self and from the self's behavior. For Sartre, *le conscient* is always present in our behavior, but not necessarily *le connu*. The new critic is precisely concerned with discovering *le connu*, all that which can be known concerning a man's behavior. He is concerned, as if he were a psychoanalyst, with the concealed, and often deeply concealed, motivations that explain human behavior.

The new critic tends to distrust and circumvent what is obvious in a work, what is clearly expressed, such as the narrative element if the book is a novel, or the ideology if the book is a play. The moral basis is particularly avoided so that all of the critic's time may be spent on a study of the obscure zones of a writer's sensitivity, of his obsessions. Thus Jean Starobinski, in studying Rousseau, tends to pass over the social ideology of the writer in order to devote his attention to Rousseau's personal drama revealed in his relationships with other people.

It has been said that all of modern criticism is "structuralist." By the word "structure," as applied to criticism, is meant not only the visible organization of the work, but the invisible, the inner and psychological architecture of the human experience out of which the writing comes. It is criticism of the work's totality, not one part of which can be understood without reference to the whole. In a complex reciprocal relationship, the part illuminates the whole, as each sentence, each word in fact, illuminates the entire work. Each sentence bears the meaning of the work, as the heart, a single organ, sustains the life of the entire body.

In a literary sense, our age is characterized by the number of books written about books. In dedicating his book to his wife, one of our best American critics wrote, "to the critic of a critic of critics." Not merely a man of discernment and taste, the critic today is called upon to be an aesthetician, a psychologist, a sociologist, a historian. The critics of each generation pass and are interred as quickly as most of its novelists and playwrights and poets. Few survive for long the rapid turnover of each decade, with the constant shifting of interests, the political changes, the scientific discoveries. Very few critics survive by imposing their methods of criticism even on one decade, and by the continuing originality of their work. Few survive as securely as Albert Thibaudet, for example, who in the 1930's was the almost official critic of *La Nouvelle revue française* and whose articles helped to place whatever author he was considering in the appropriate context of literary history. The articles of Maurice Blanchot, published during the 1950's in *La Nouvelle revue française,* are very different from those of Thibaudet, but they too seem destined to last for some time, by the serious questions they raise concerning the basic assumptions of literature, concerning the very reasons for having books at all and having readers of these books.

Our age is one of literary inflation and of great confusion of values. A great deal is being written, a great deal is being published, and a great deal is being written on what is published. One often has the impression that too much talent is ascribed to second-rate writers and that genius is too easily ascribed to talented writers. What is apparently new in literature (the French use the word *actuel* for this) is often hailed as important and significant and the critic is often deceived by what he looks upon as enduring qualities of the new. A new writer has to be judged not only by the intensity with which he lives the present moment of history, but also by the way in which he demonstrates resourcefulness in facing the future. Is it possible to judge such matters at the time of the first publication of a book? What guides the critic in his evaluations? It has to do, in some way or other, with the relationship an author establishes between himself and the world. It has to do with the quality of this relationship. Charles Du Bos was able to see it immediately in Proust, and Jacques Rivière saw it immediately in Claudel.

The new critics seem to agree that the skill of pleasing the reader no longer counts in literature. Some will even go so far as to say that the type of writing called literature is tending to disappear. The future belongs to nonliterary literature. The specifically literary quality of Sartre's writing, for example, is weak. His own use of the word "literature" in his famous essay represents a radical change in meaning. The entire concept of literature may be engaged at this moment in a more serious crisis than even the new critics realize. It may be a crisis endangering the very existence of literature. And such a crisis, if the word is not too flamboyant, engages all of man and all of his activities.

During the experience of reading any one of the new critics, whether it be Barthes or Goldmann or Mauron, the reader feels that the critic is more important than the subject of his criticism. The critic today has learned how to impose himself as a writer. His work is something that exists in addition to the work that is being criticized. It is not merely a reflection of the work, or a commentary on the work. It has its own strength by representing an exclusive viewpoint, although this viewpoint opens out to many horizons. The study of the new critic centers on the belief that a literary work is essentially ambiguous, that a literary work says more than the writer meant to say and often says something different from what he thought he said.

7

Surrealist and Psychoanalytical Criticism

The richest years of surrealism were those between 1925 and 1935, when the leading figures of the movement questioned all the traditional values and forms of literature. They pointed out the failure of bourgeois society to bring happiness and freedom to man. They pointed out the emphasis Freud had made on man not essentially the reasoner, but man the sleeper and the dreamer. In their attacks on the novel as a literary genre, the surrealists stressed the falseness of realist observation, the logical fabrication of plot, the absence of inquiry into any of the real mysteries of life. Surrealism was to be a new conquest of the world and of man's mind, a new fusion of reality and dreams.

There had been literary ancestors in this way of apprehending reality, and the surrealists of the 1920's were eager to acknowledge and approve publicly of these forerunners, and thereby eager to deride many of the traditional well-established literary figures. They praised the Gothic tale of the eighteenth century: Horace Walpole, Ann Radcliffe, Maturin, Lewis, and especially the writings of the Marquis de Sade. They rediscovered certain romantic writers who had been seriously neglected: Aloysius Bertrand, Pétrus Borel, Gérard de Nerval. From Baudelaire's work, they chose the *poèmes en prose* for special commendation, because of the poetry he had discovered in the usual aspects of daily life and transcribes in his fifty prose poems. The works of Lautréamont, Rimbaud, and Jarry also were admitted to the category of presurrealist works. In the writings of such authors, by associations of words one with the other and by juxtapositions, the subconscious is liberated. This liberation of the subconscious in the creating of literature was always associated by the surrealists with the concept of liberty they found in the new political doctrine of Marxism.

The first book of literary criticism that attempted to trace this development from the prose poems of Baudelaire to the major writings of the surrealists, appeared in 1933, *De Baudelaire au surréalisme*, by Marcel Raymond. Today this book is esteemed more highly than ever as a pioneer critical text where surrealist traits of the poets studied: Baudelaire, the symbolists, Apollinaire, Jacob, Reverdy, are explained by a quasi-psychoanalytical method. Two other books of the same decade, *L'Echec de Baudelaire* (1931) by René Laforgue and *Edgar Poe* (1933) by Marie Bonaparte (a French disciple of Freud), are studies closer to medicine than literary criticism. Both Laforgue and Bonaparte look upon a literary work as an expression of the pathological subconscious. In the preface to *Edgar Poe*, written by Freud himself, a key acknowledgment is made by the scientist when he says that the kind of research carried out by Mme Bonaparte, does not pretend to explain a literary genius but to point out those factors that awakened the genius and the subject matter which his fate of a genius imposed upon him. *De telles recherches ne prétendent pas expliquer le génie des créateurs, mais elles montrent quels facteurs lui ont donné l'éveil et quelle sorte de matière lui est imposée par le destin.*

The way, opened up by Marcel Raymond, was continued by Gaston Bachelard whose contribution to psychoanalytical criticism is among the most notable. In his close analysis of the writings of the poets, he tries to discover the relationship between the recurring images in the poems and the dream world of the poet, the oneiric reality, as he calls it. Then he studies the relationship existing between the images of the poet and the elements of fire, air, water, land. Bachelard's many volumes are studies of the dynamic character of the poet's imagination. The first volume was devoted to fire, *Psychanalyse du feu* (1937); the second to water, *L'Eau et les rêves* (1942); and the third to air, *L'Air et les songes* (1943). Bachelard, like Marcel Raymond before him, sought to relive the inner life of the writer and thereby rediscover the first, the primitive experiences that preside over the literary work.

To the names of Raymond and Bachelard should be added that of Albert Béguin, who in an important study of 1937, *L'Ame romantique et le rêve*, combined a psychoanalytical with a metaphysical exploration of certain key poetic figures who have counted not only in romanticism but in the post-romantic period.

These were the three masters of the method, and their influence and example continued to count for subsequent critics whose method is largely psychoanalytical: Georges Blin in his study of Baudelaire and his two studies of Stendhal where Stendhal is seen to be the analyst of himself in his writings; Georges Poulet in such books as *Les Métamorphoses du cercle* and *L'Espace proustien*, where the critic tries always to return to the basic situation from which the writer took his start; Sartre's studies of Baudelaire and Genet; Jean-Pierre Richard who in his analysis of Mallarmé's work considers the poet's contact with the world (*L'Univers imaginaire de Mallarmé*, 1962); Jean Rousset who develops the thesis that a writer does not write in order to say something, but writes in order to narrate himself; Charles Mauron who in his last book, *Des métaphores obsédantes au mythe personnel*, combines psychoanalytical interpretation with biography and thematic analysis.

Psychoanalysis has never been one school. And yet, certain basic concepts do provide a unity joining the several schools. Those literary critics, attracted by the method of psychoanalysis, are fully aware of the widely accepted beliefs and practices on which the method is based.

Four or five fundamental concepts of psychoanalysis are clearly visible in literary criticism that reflects psychoanalysis. The thought and the sentiments of a man at any one moment of his life depend upon the entire history of his personal motivation, and the way in which he considers and judges his surroundings. A man's early childhood is of great importance in the forming and development of his personality. This second belief has to do with the man's instinctive tenderness when he was a child and the effect on it of the pychological-social structure of his environment. It involves therefore a man's conscious perceptions and his inner reactions of guilt and inhibitions. A third belief is the importance in a man's psychic life of his frustrations, even if these frustrations are often sublimated and rationalized. His unawareness, at least his conscious unawareness of these conflicts is significant enough to be classified as a fourth belief. When a man writes, he expresses the psychological results of his life and the causes of his behavior, but he does not express the latent power of frustrations and inner conflicts. Literary psychoanalysis tries precisely to define the latent psychic content of a work.

Otto Rank in his book on incest in literature (*Le Thème de l'inceste dans la poésie et les contes,* 1911), Laforgue in his book on Baudelaire, and Bonaparte in her work on Poe are more concerned with the analysis of neuroticism (*névrose*) as it occurs in literature than with any critical appreciation. The real founder of psychoanalytical criticism was Charles Baudouin in his two books, *Psychanalyse de l'art* (1929) and *Psychanalyse de Victor Hugo* (1943). He used psychiatry for an interpretation and an appreciation of literature, and this method was continued by Mauron in his *Introduction àla psychanalyse de Mallarmé,* (1950). Mauron studied the texts of the poet and biographical data in order to reconstruct his fundamental complexes. Bachelard also followed this method in his book *Lautréamont* (1939), in his psychoanalysis of fire, and in his last book, *La Poétique de la rêverie* (1960). Whereas Bonaparte's approach was an analysis of the work of the poet in order to understand the man, Bachelard's approach began with the work in order to explain the man, and then returned to the work as the real goal of his inquiry.

The wisest of the psychoanalytical critics, a Baudouin and a Mauron, never confine their explanation of an author to a single psychic phenomenon as it can be observed in a poet. Hugo's guilt is never thus analyzed by Baudouin, and Mallarmé's memory of his dead sister is never thus used by Mauron. However, these critics claim that Hugo and Mallarmé would not have written in the way they did without those experiences. In other words, the secretive, the unconscious obsession of a dead sister suggested to Mallarmé a certain choice of images that are in his poems. Bachelard studied those images in a poet's work that he believed corresponded to the reality of the poet's imagination. He explains that a man's mind, as it contemplates matter, as it contemplates any one of the four elements of the universe, is hungry to discover those images that will satisfy the hunger and that bear relationship with the deep, the oneiric images of a universal archetype.

The influence of Charles Mauron, who died at the end of 1966, will doubtless be far-reaching in the present and the next generation of French critics. In his first three books—*Mallarmé l'obscur* (1941), *Introduction à la psychanalyse de Mallarmé* (1950), and *L'Inconscient dans l'oeuvre et la vie de Racine* (1957)—and in his recent book, *Des métaphores obsédantes au mythe personnel* (1963), where he studies Baudelaire, Nerval, Mallarmé, and Valéry from the viewpoint of the subconscious of metaphorical analogies, Mauron raises the question of how much knowledge we can obtain from a work of art by a scientific, psychological, and anthropological method. Psychoanalytical criticism never eludes this question. Mauron believes that a scientific inquiry never embraces the essential knowledge of a work of art. The writer is always surpassed by his writing. That is why the secret of the poets is always well guarded. But psychoanalytical

criticism can teach us how to recognize the functioning of
the poet and the way in which he writes.

The type of criticism which Mauron produced involves
a vast amount of philosophical, psychological, and phe-
nomenological information which constructs around a
given work of art a closely woven network of analyses,
allusions, and theories. In his exegesis he deploys an amaz-
ing dialectical virtuosity. Mauron's Sorbonne doctoral dissertation, *Des métaphores obsédantes au mythe personnel*,
is a long work crammed with quotations, analyses, and
ideas. He calls his method *la psychocritique* in order to
distinguish it from the "thematic" criticism of Poulet,
Richard, and Starobinski.

Psychocriticism consists in detecting in a literary work
"families" (*familles*) or what Mauron prefers to call "networks or "clusters" (*réseaux*) of obsessive images. His
hypothesis states that those images or signs come from the
writer's subconscious and furnish the principal elements
of his style. They are more vital, more decisive than
those images that seem to come from the writer's environment or culture, from historical or exterior sources.
The images that rise up from the most obscure sources
of the personality reveal the fundamental intention of
a work. Mauron insists that the investigations of the
"thematic" critics are radically different from his. In
studying the *thèmes structurels* of a work, the critic is still
concerned with the consciousness of the writer and there
the method of psychoanalysis is not always applied. He,
on the contrary, is concerned with an obsession foreign to
the conscious will of the artist where images are less
precise, less clear, and are formed by groups of associations
(*réseaux d'associations*). In such automatic associations,
the writer's thought is primitive, antedating logic, using
those images that have a strong emotional charge.

At times it is difficult to distinguish between "theme"
or the conscious elaboration of a form, and an "obsessive
image" or one appearing in a pure or primitive state. And
when all is said, Mauron's explanations of Mallarmé's
images seem just as arbitrary as those of Richard. The line

of demarcation between the conscious and the subconscious is often difficult to ascertain. The basic hypothesis of Mauron's method is at times hard to justify—namely, the importance he gives to the subconsciously chosen image. And yet parts of the hypothesis are brilliantly conceived.

The metaphor is first produced by the demands of the mind which has something to say, something to express, and then in the creation of the metaphor, images or analogies rise up from a subconscious chaos. From ten passages of Baudelaire's poems and prose poems, Mauron discusses a network of metaphors (*réseau de métaphores*) all suggesting heaviness, a weight felt on the neck or shoulders of the poet. The heavy weight that Sisyphus lifts (*un poids si lourd*), the weight of Jeanne's hair (*le poids de la chevelure*), the chimera, as heavy as a bag of flour (*une chimère aussi lourde qu'un sac de farine*—for all of these images of weight, Mauron finds a source in a nightmare Baudelaire had and which he related in letters. As the heaviness grows, Mauron believes it ends by becoming the weight of destiny and the final obsession with the tomb. Such a cluster of images would therefore come from a congenital disposition governing the poet's subconscious.

At the time of Mauron's death, his last book appeared, *Le Dernier Baudelaire*, a defense, with illustrations, of his psychocritic method. He limits himself to one text, the *Petits poèmes en prose*. The analyst in his office can follow the free associations of his patient, associations which the analyst himself solicits. The critic substitutes for that method an association of passages from the author in question, patiently collected and grouped together as evidence of related themes, images, metaphors that reveal important constructions of the subconscious. In this kind of research, Mauron claims he is using scientific objectivity. On this claim he has been attacked by such different critics as Raymond Picard and Serge Doubrovsky. In a note in this small book, *Le Dernier Baudelaire*, Mauron replies to his critics by saying they have not read his writings carefully, or they have misread them. His psychocriticism is intended to be partial or tentative and not absolutistic. His analysis is concerned with the subconscious structures of the writers he studies, but these writers also have conscious structures. In an important sentence of self-defense, Mauron says that the participation of the subconscious in literary creation is of an oneiric preverbal order: *La participation de l'inconscient à la création est d'ordre onirique, donc préverbale.*

Mauron's method is luminously clear in *Le Dernier Baudelaire.* It is a process of gradual illumination of the way in which a text came to be written, but it is not the imposing of one interpretation or one point of view on the text. For the elaboration of his method Mauron never relinquished the belief that Baudelaire in his life and Baudelaire as a writer shared the same subconscious state. From 1861 on, Baudelaire was obsessed with a set of preoccupations, of fantasies and anguish and dreams that belonged to his social self as well as to his creative self. Mauron undertook the study of the relationship between these two selves. Other critics of Baudelaire had attempted this—Georges Blin, Sartre, Michel Butor—but no one of them has so painstakingly emphasized the role of money, of material insecurity, of the financial arrangements with Ancelle and Caroline Aupick, that tormented Baudelaire at the time he was writing *Le Spleen de Paris.* Baudelaire's worry over poverty and his prodigality are analyzed by Mauron as the foundation of his particular tragic world. Such worries, united with those he had known as a child, form, for the critic, a "protopoem" on which the poet drew for his inspiration. By means of this scrutiny and analysis, certain of the *petits poèmes en prose* reveal "structures" that had not been seen heretofore: *Le Vieux saltimbanque, Les Veuves, Le Fou et la Vénus,* among others.

Half of Gaston Bachelard's books (he had published more than thirty before his death in 1963, at the age of seventy-nine) are difficult books on the history and the philosophy of science. The others are easier to read, but they are read

especially by writers and critics, some of whom—Roland
Barthes and Jean-Pierre Richard in particular—have acknowledged the debt they owe them. It is not exaggerated
to say that Gaston Bachelard founded a literary fashion in
French letters, a way of speaking about literature. He is
primarily a philosopher, with a solid training in the sciences. (In this regard, he is not unlike Teilhard de Chardin.) This second part of his career was largely devoted to
a study of the poetic imagination, or that part of human
nature that is hardest for science to approach. His understanding of literary and scientific themes was the basis of
his Sorbonne lectures. He was appointed to a professorship at the age of fifty-six. He delighted and inspired his
students by his generosity and wisdom during his lectures
and after the lectures when he often joined them at a
Latin Quarter café.

Bachelard profited from his students. He was able to
put them at ease by his cordiality and simple manners,
and they spoke freely with him. In fact, it was to some
degree their criticism of him at Dijon where he was a
university teacher that helped to modify his career. He
overheard the phrase, said by a student, *l'univers pasteu-
risé de Bachelard*, and decided to change the careful presentation of his lectures from which all microbes had been
eliminated. The change in his thinking and critical approach was first apparent in *La Psychanalyse du feu*. One
of his last books, published in 1961, *La Flamme d'une
chandelle*, is also on the element of fire, on the spirituality
of candlelight as opposed to the sexual force of fire.

Bachelard's attitude toward the imagination accounts
for a shift from a psychoanalytical approach, clearly visible
in his first volumes on the elements, to a phenomenolog-
ical approach in his later books. The imagination, rather
than being one individual's experiences, may be reduced
to a series of experiences. Bachelard substantiates these
principles with a large number of quotations taken from
many literary sources. Science has become so complex
today that it cannot keep up with its discoveries and with
its own philosophy. Therefore the imagination cannot

find a refuge in science. To science Bachelard opposes the
subject matter of poetry, namely the imagination which,
as far back as we can go in history, has looked upon a
flame as an image of passionate love. Such an image as a
flame is used by the poets primarily because it is also used
by daydreamers. The habit of daydreaming, of fantasy-
making, is considered by Bachelard as a normal healthy
exercise of the psyche. He distinguishes between daydreaming or *la rêverie* and *le rêve* or dreams that occur
during a man's sleep.

In order to develop a resilient psyche, man has to develop a sound relationship between himself and the outside world. This comes about in the most natural way
possible when man allows his mind to dwell half-
consciously on sensations of color and movement, forms
and textures. This habit of daydreaming is the way the
material world penetrates the inner life of a man. These
sensations are the substance of poems, and they occur also
in philosophies and novels and essays. Bachelard's critical
work is an effort to systematize the sensations.

In his analysis of these sensations as they appear in
poetry, Bachelard develops a form of hygiene which he
proposes to his readers. The most famous example in his
work is the importance for a man to have in his home an
open wood fire (see *La Psychanalyse du feu*). The fire is
of course useful in itself, in providing heat, but it also
provides a picture of sexuality. A man's eyes need this urge
to sexual life as he sits in front of the fire. These sensations of sight and warmth are teachers of sexual love. In
another book, *La Poétique de l'espace*, there is a further
image connected with the home, which is not as famous as
the open fire. It is the importance of having a cellar and
an attic in one's house. The cellar represents the subconscious, the dark hidden forces in us, and the attic represents our need for spiritual elevation. The two images
taken together form Bachelard's advice never to live in a
centrally heated apartment where we are not able to enjoy
an open fire and the possession of a cellar and an attic. If
we are forced by circumstances to live in such a restricted

way, our one recourse is daydreaming about a more ideal home where we can enjoy the play of flames in a fireplace and the knowledge that there are secret spaces above us and below us. Such a psychoanalyst as Bachelard will make no distinction between the habits of daydreaming and the habits of daily living.

In his critical writing, Bachelard is something of a philosopher and something of a poet. He says that the two poles of man's psychic life are the intellect and the imagination. The intellect exists for the creation of concepts, and the imagination for the creation of images. Bachelard has called them the male and female poles of the psyche.

Psychoanalysis, in the domain of literary creation, was originally concerned only with the genesis of a work. It sought to demonstrate how much a literary work owed to the richness of the writer's subconscious. Freud claimed that a work translates a primitive infantile desire of the writer that had been repressed by the process of growing up and adjusting to society. But these subconsciously repressed desires, when articulated by a writer, must be susceptible of being shared and recognized by other men. Psychoanalysis, especially in its literary context, has always stressed such universal polarizations as the Oedipus complex, the fear of castration, the libido, infantile egoism, rivalry between brothers, and the dread of death. The emotional forces of such structures as these belong more to the collective subconscious than to the subconscious of an individual. Freud, Jung, Bachelard, and their disciples have continued to study the power of images, especially those from dreams and myths, as containing the clue to man's most fundamental instincts, as images related to the most obscure drives of our existence.

Psychoanalysis originally argued that man's complexes and obsessions give meaning to the images of his dreams and his literary creations. Bachelard has added the further argument that the function of images, in a poem for example, is to restore its full power to a complex. The complex, or the archetypal obsession, since it is subconscious, cannot be articulated in any direct or literary form. It has to be translated and decodified by the analyst.

In his book, *L'Eau et les rêves*, Bachelard studies the element of water as it is expressed in the myth of Narcissus. As the boy bends over the water and sees all of nature reflected in it, the presence of so profound a substance, of so universal and unchangeable a substance as water, captivates all of his power of dreaming, and he indulges in the sentiments of security and eternity. The role of the psychoanalyst is to explain the meaning of this sentiment. Water in a state of calm evokes woman and nudity. When imaginatively we think of a person emerging from water, we think of her without hair and without clothes on her body. She is first an image, first a desire, before being a person. Why is this? Water is related to woman and to birth, to woman in her role of mother. Water is the source of life, the nourishment of life.

Dreams, where the image of water dominates, are concerned, first, with birth and, secondly, with death. What is visible on water is a reflection and therefore constantly under the threat of disappearing. So, the contemplation of water can also be a meditation on one's fate to dissolve and die. Narcissus, at the beginning of his self-contemplation, feels secure with the presence of water, with its depth and peacefulness, but this sentiment changes in time to one of dark foreboding when he realizes that water, as night falls, absorbs the dark and changes into a hard compact substance. Water is the source of images: of all those that signify, first, security and peacefulness, and then of all those that signify a threat to the life of man. It may first call to mind a need to return to man's prenatal state when he lived in the waters of the womb, and it may then remind man of what is to come in his human experience, his burial in mother earth, which will be, in a sense, a new birth.

Water is thus the image of two psychological needs of man, related to birth and death, and which are perhaps the same need. Bachelard reminds us that burial, for some prehistoric peoples, was the placing of the body in a hollowed-out tree which was then set afloat and abandoned. In analyzing this ritual, he calls it the complex of Charon the boatman in hell, and the complex of Ophelia, where water is the element yearned for. Water is for Ophelia the synthesis of woman and death.

Whether water be the desire for life or for death, it is related to one of the most insistent and one of the most deep-seated instincts of man. Bachelard's role of critic is to interpret this image as it occurs in literature. Every image, for Bachelard, which implies one of the original elements—fire, air, water, earth—is a mask concealing a basic need of man. The critic reexamines all the forms of matter in their relationships with human passions, needs, and instinctual drives. This is why Bachelard insists that dreams connected with matter (with the elements) are more significant than dreams connected merely with objects.

Bachelard never denies the complexity of such myths as Narcissus and his fountain, of the bather emerging naked from the water, of Ophelia's death by drowning, of Charon's boat in the river of hell, of Leda and the swan. They are related to prenatal security, to erotic desire, to fear and yearning for death. But all of these experiences or obsessions are perhaps more closely related than one realizes. Attraction and repulsion may not be so far apart as one thinks. The study of such images tends to rob them of their mystery, of their morbidity, of the strangeness of their fascination. They are not always what they appear to be. They are images of metamorphosis. Venus as she rises up nude from the sea may be something else than an image of woman. Bachelard is fully aware that the psychoanalysis of an image will break its power of an obsession. Psychoanalysis is fundamentally iconoclastic, in the etymological sense of image-destroyer. In its therapeutic role of healer, psychoanalysis dissipates the image and therefore the complex. But if the image is that of a primordial organic element of man, as it becomes clear for us, our fascination with it may well increase.

If, for example, water is evocative of birth, it is because all of us were originally born out of the depths of the sea. Bachelard's method is based upon his belief that all of man's basic psychological realities are manifested by images. His role is that of interpreter of those images which by their very nature conceal their reality and their meaning. The elements react on the imagination of a man because that is his image-making faculty.

This method goes very far in explaining, or rather reexplaining the reason for and the function of poetry. What is poetry if it is not the manifestation, by means of images and sound, of forces that are invisible and soundless? When Bachelard speaks of the earliest kind of poetry we know, he calls it a clinging to the invisible (*l'adhésion à l'invisible*). By "invisible" he means reality beyond the reality of images. If mankind tends to think of Eve as a beautiful woman, as Venus or as Mary, it is not because she was born from one of Adam's ribs, but because, as Bachelard pointedly and movingly says, she was born from one of Adam's dreams. Water is a significant element for the poet, not only because it is able to reflect the exterior beauty of the world, but also because it is able to reflect the poet's imagination, all the images his mind creates.

Poetry in its pristine etymological sense is something that is made, something that is made real. Bachelard will go so far as to claim that this image-making power of the poet antedates his emotions. If Freud emphasizes complexes in his psychoanalytical method, and Jung emphasizes archetypes in his, Bachelard emphasizes the four elements and images related to the elements. But all three analysts, in their study of complexes, archetypes, and elements, are concerned with the symbolization of the fundamental tendencies in man which are repeated from century to century: man's need to dominate (*libido dominandi*), his sexual desires (*libido sentiendi*), his yearning for knowledge (*libido sciendi*), his fear of being closed in, his fear of death, his longing for freedom. Images as they occur in art, in myths, and in dreams are the same. But the language of art, whether it be an ode of Claudel or a tragedy of Sophocles; and the story in which a myth is articulated: Charon's boat ride or the search for self in the fountain of Narcissus; and the persistent images that return nightly in a man's dreams—all of these exist by themselves, intact and unassailable, as part of the legacies that have come down to us. The labors of the critic would not be understood without such legacies because he would not attempt to interpret what does not already exist in art, in myths, and in dreams.

In the new terminology of the critic, what are "structures," as they appear in dreams and myths and art? What would be some of the examples? They might be the image of flight in a dream, the unusually vain effort to escape from some pursuer; or the pitiful story of the infant-boy Oedipus abandoned and exposed on a mountainside; or the monstrousness of the white sperm whale Moby Dick; or the two ways in Proust's novel, Swann's way and Guermantes' way, or the phantomlike picture of Mallarmé's swan caught in the frozen lake. The variety of these images is endless, and yet they are all familiar to us, even if we have never lived on a whaling vessel or seen in the north a frozen lake.

These are random examples of structures. They have one thing in common, whether they come from dreams or myths or novels: they are dissimulations. They are structures that hide something. This principle of concealment and mystery explains the fascination they exert over us. It is why we decide to dream them over again every night. It is why we reread *Wuthering Heights* every year. It is why we memorize *Among School Children* of Yeats, because we are never sure of who those schoolchildren are. It is why we return three or four times to see such films as *Blowup* by Antonioni, *Julietta and the Spirits of* Fellini, and *The Servant* by Losey. In such works of art that epitomize the mysteries of life and dreams, we can never be absolutely sure of what the young man is trying to photograph, of what is going on in Julietta's mind, and of what secret power the servant wants to manipulate.

The literary psychoanalyst knows that we live in a world of mirrors. Each of us is reflected in the dreams we have at night and the half-consciously willed dreams we have as we watch the burning logs of a fire or the waves as they continue to roll in and break on the seashore. Each of us is reflected in those mythic stories that have held us from childhood, held us because they have never been totally comprehensible: the flight of the boy Icarus whose wings gave way as he mounted toward the sun, or those flights of Superman, more successful than Icarus, in a new world of science; the man who lives alone in nature and who is able to communicate with animals: Saint Francis of Assisi, or Robinson on his island, or Tarzan in his jungle; the metamorphosis of Cinderella, or Dr. Jekyll, or the beast who is a prince, or the rod that Moses turned into a serpent. The literary analyst knows that each of these metamorphoses represents a complex constituting the very being of man. It is at the origins of those archetypal patterns we call tendencies and impulses in man. If we could understand the complex, it would help to explain the ambiguous situation where each of us lives in the world.

The domain of beauty (which we call aesthetics) and the domain of knowledge (which we call science) are both invaded by the literary analyst. His search is an adventure, almost a perilous adventure, where he half sees truths that seem to belong to some other domain beyond aesthetics and science. Some of the ultimate discoveries of Bachelard would seem to point toward an almost terrifying definition of man. He would seem to be that being for whom truth means the avoidance of reaching the ultimate truth. He is that being who wills not to be known, who prefers to pursue his existence within the images of dreams and myths and art, who accepts the strangeness of these images and their limitless possibilities, and who does not want a total liberation from them.

Georges Bataille (1897–1962) underwent psychoanalysis in 1926 and 1927 at the end of a period of depression and turmoil. In 1929 he helped to found an art magazine *Documents* which was hostile to André Breton and which welcomed those surrealists who had separated at that time from Breton: Michel Leiris, André Masson, Desnos, Vitrac, and others. Bataille was denounced by Breton in the *Second manifeste du surréalisme* (published first in *La Révolution surréaliste* in 1929). By the time *Documents* ceased being published, in 1931, most of the early opponents of Breton had returned to him. Bataille had been reconciled with Breton at the time of his magazine *Acéphale*, which in its four issues between 1936 and 1939 expressed his Nietzschean antireligious views. Two of his principal books were written in the early forties: *L'Expérience intérieure* (1943) and *Sur Nietzsche* (1945). From Vézelay, where he lived from 1942 on, after retiring from a post at the Bibliothèque nationale because of tuberculosis, Bataille founded in 1941 with the collaboration of Eric Weil and Jean Piel the important magazine *Critique*. *La Part maudite* (1949) is the first *vue d'ensemble* of Bataille's thought. *L'Érotisme* and *La Littérature et le mal* are the fullest development of his thought concerning the theme to which he had made the most significant contribution: the role of eroticism in literature.

La Littérature et le mal is a collection of essays which had first appeared in *Critique*. *L'Érotisme* is a long documented essay on the same subject, with appended articles and lectures. They are meditations on the practice of literature and gravitate around the essential theme of man's fate. Bataille analyzes human conduct as it differs from the habits of animals and offers a picture of man as he should be, a human vocation which would reveal the real value of man.

The title *L'Érotisme* is ill-chosen, because it would seem to indicate that sexuality is at the basis of human behavior. Bataille is actually opposed to such a theory and criticizes such a French disciple of Freud as Marie Bonaparte in her attempt to interpret every mystical experience as a disguised sexual experience. Bataille tries to discover a common goal for all human experiences which are particularly intense. He defines this goal as the change from a discontinuity of behavior which characterizes human behavior to a continuity which will reconcile a human being with other human beings and offer him some form of happiness. Although he seems to indicate that such a reconciliation is impossible, Bataille suggests that, if it does come about, it will follow trials and experiences that are comparable to death itself.

Eroticism occupies the central position in the essay, because man's sexual experience is seen by Bataille to be the surest means he has to become that kind of being he longs to become. Bataille studies other human experiences, such as war, sacrifice, and mysticism, in their relationship with eroticism. When Bataille argues that life in its fundamental drives is violent, he recalls Nietzsche. The taboos and prohibitions of society all aim at suppressing or denouncing the excessive manifestations of life which precisely are violent. In the heart of a man a constant struggle is going on between anguish instituted by prohibitions, and the desire to transgress, to perform some act of violence. But the notion of the sacred rises up with the violation of law, with transgression itself. War goes counter to the law against killing, and war in its origins at least has a strong element of the sacred. Today in our secularized world, war may conceal man's fundamental desire to destroy and enjoy an experience of violence which is a fundamental drive of life.

Society's prohibition against erotic practices has a similar goal of opposing waste and violence. Eroticism is the desire to move beyond the boundaries of ordinary life, to know a mystical experience that is comparable to death in the sense that it transports man beyond the familiar. It is highly significant that the orgasm or climax of sexual love is often referred to as the "little death." The seriousness attached to this act, in society, comes from the fact that it is a violation of law, an indulgence in something that is prohibited. But this very prohibition, as Baudelaire has pointed out in a famous sentence, adds intensity and a fundamental pleasure to the sexual act. Voluptuousness comes from the knowledge that one is doing something evil. The ceremony of marriage legalizes for society the sexual act, and Bataille interprets this as acknowledgment that society cannot totally suppress irrational violence, that it tolerates it somewhat, in order to impose other major limitations. If Bataille's theory is sound, it follows that the pleasure accompanying the sexual act is greater outside of marriage.

Mystics themselves have pointed out analogies between an erotic experience and a mystical experience. Both, in their attainment to ecstasy, are seen to be efforts to move beyond the limitations ordinarily imposed on human life. Although Christianity has never been hostile to religious ecstasy, it has often been distrustful of it. Implied in this distrust, is the general law of man not to move outside of the norm of life, not to indulge in the use of drugs, for example, that would lead man to regions outside of life and death. But every great human passion, expressed in literature, is described in that way, as a means of moving beyond the usual limitations of existence.

This is the central thesis of Bataille's *La Littérature et le mal,* namely the guilt of literature, the defense of evil which the greatest writers have assumed. In his chapters on Emily Brontë, Baudelaire, Proust, Michelet, Sade, Genet, the thesis and the conclusion of the thesis are the same: the major writers of the world affirm both the need for law and restrictions, and the need to violate the law and transgress the restrictions. Good and evil are complementary. In his most deeply spiritual experiences, man revindicates his fundamental guilt. One of the clearest examples Bataille studies is that of *Wuthering Heights* which he interprets as Emily Brontë's impassioned attack against a world governed by law, against the good. Heathcliff is the rebellious boy who never forgave Cathy for betraying her child's world and going over to the side of the defenders of the law. Man's freedom, according to Bataille, is best affirmed in his practice and in his praise of evil. The will to move outside of laws and restrictions is the experience of man's sovereignty.

In the analysis of this thought, Bataille draws heavily upon the philosophy of Nietzsche and his interpretation of the sacred in human life. The concept of sovereignty is accompanied by a need to communicate the concept. Bataille uses this theory to explain the case of Jean Genet. He draws constantly upon religious motives of sin in order to define the prestige of transgressions. He is close to Baudelaire's theology when he claims that man discovers the sense of the sacred when he commits transgressions. Bataille's thought often seems to be confusedly atheistic and Jansenistic. The noblest inclinations of man, as well as his most erotic pleasures, are determined by the force and the attraction of evil.

Bataille, as an essayist who moves between the domains of sociology and mysticism, often gives the impression of suffering acutely with and through the ideas he tries to express. The form his writing usually takes is a series of brief developments, almost fragments. They often seem to be broken off when their intensity is too great to be sustained. Behind the aphorisms and the *pensées* of Nietzsche and Pascal, one senses the existence of a plan, of a coherent dialectic. Bataille's fragments do not give the impression that behind them the writer is constructing a system. The fragments are the complete communication. They are the experience he is seeking to reveal. Bataille's inner experience (*expérience intérieure*) cannot be communicated as a form of knowledge. He is not looking for a vision of the world that will contain and surpass all contradictions, in which he would resemble such writers as Nietzsche and Pascal. He is seeking an experience which itself is a unity, which itself is a source. The words he uses to describe this experience are all approximate: "inner," "sovereign," "ecstatic," "erotic." Whether Bataille calls this experience *érotisme* or *ivresse* or *poésie* or *sacrifice*, he means it as a total experience that liberates man from the usual reality that can be divided and dissected and analyzed.

Most activities of man prepare the future. They prepare matters that will serve in the future. Bataille understood another kind of experience—which he calls "eroticism," for example—that will permit man to live totally in the present moment. It is an experience that will not lead to something else. Emotion is a momentary experience existing for itself, a passion, a fever which does not prepare or look forward to any future result. For Bataille the great ecstatic or religious emotions of man are not very different from the emotions of madness or the emotions of love.

8

Primacy of the Text:
Thematic Criticism

Soon after the beginning of the war, in 1943 when Bataille's *Expérience intérieure* appeared, on page 158 fervent
reference was made to the critic Maurice Blanchot. He
was quite unknown at that time when Sartre and Camus
were beginning to mobilize most of the literary attention.
During the next quarter of a century, Blanchot was read,
not by the general public, but by an ever-increasing number of writers. This attention by the élite culminated in
June 1966 in an homage number of *Critique* to Blanchot
where he was celebrated in articles by René Char, Jean
Starobinski, Emmanuel Lévinas, Michel Foucault, Paul
de Man. These articles are more than homage to the critic
Maurice Blanchot, they are ways of understanding his
thought, ways of estimating his contribution to French
letters and contemporary criticism. They form a more
unified critical volume than the usual collection of homage articles. They illustrate the degree to which the
thought of Blanchot has affected his critics and interpreters. Each in his own way has been nourished and guided
by Blanchot. The reading of Blanchot's texts has been for
each of these critics more than a mere experience of
reading.

Blanchot's answer to the question, what is literature,
has become clearer with each of his major books of criticism: with *Faux pas*, published in 1943; with *La Part du
feu*, six years later, in 1949; *Lautréamont et Sade*, also in
1949; and *L'Espace littéraire*, in 1955. His principal belief
would seem to be the conviction that an authentic work of

literary criticism is an experience by which a writer enters upon an existence that he did not know before writing. The critic looks upon each work he considers as something singular, as a form that is irreducible, as a creation that comes from the author and from his moment in history, and from the literary genre of which it is representative. The critic moves from book to book, marveling at the endless variety of literature, and using comparisons in his art of critic as generously as a poet uses metaphors.

In his first collection of articles, *Faux pas*, Blanchot analyzes the work of Albert Thibaudet who in many ways was his predecessor. At several points in the article, as Blanchot analyzes the method of Thibaudet, he seems to be analyzing his own method, or at least his method at the beginning of his career. Although Thibaudet did stress the uniqueness of a work of art, he inevitably defined it in terms of the historical period when it was created. A literary work is looked upon by Blanchot as something separated from its age, as *un monde à part*, as a solitary secret. Already in *Faux pas*, Blanchot in his critical method chose to consider a literary work as anonymous, whereas the ordinary critic, even in discussing a work's singularity and originality, attaches it to a historical situation and to a biography.

From the earliest articles of Blanchot, it was clear that his criticism was not going to be a critical analysis of a work, but that it was to be, in some form or other, a philosophy of literature. He is not so much concerned with the analysis of a given text—in fact he appears almost impatient with such matters which at times he cannot avoid—as with the prevailing problem of why such a text came into being in the first place. Why is there literature? How can one explain the phenomenon of a book? Why is there an author of a book? Why is there a reader of a book? How is literature possible?

Such questions as these become the leading points of departure in the articles of *La Part du feu*. Blanchot concentrates the problem of how a critic can explain the paradoxes and ambiguities prevalent in every book, prevalent in the reasons for a book being written. How can a man write such a sentence as "I am wretched" (*Je suis malheureux*) when, by writing it, he is recovering from the state of wretchedness and establishing a communion and a friendship with a reader? To raise such questions and to discuss them, Blanchot needs to have books to read and consider. From the contemporary output of books, he chose the best, with an extraordinary flair for the best. In the articles of *La Part du feu*, he discusses the first books of Camus and Audiberti, of Sartre and Queneau, of Ponge, Michaux and Char. In a word, Blanchot chose those texts which go to the heart of the questions that preoccupy him, that raise cogently the entire *raison d'être* for literature: the paradox of literature, the basic reasons for writing a book.

Blanchot refuses to believe that the critic has an edge on the book he is criticizing, that he is more learned than the book and the book's author. Blanchot would claim that the modern critic does not pretend to explain how a book is written or how a masterpiece should be written. In *Lautréamont et Sade* Blanchot says that a critic's task is to show how a given work, already written and published, was impossible to write. Critics tend to discuss a book in terms of its beauty, in terms of the culture it represents, in terms of the truth it reflects. But Blanchot tries to show how the reality of a book lies beyond all such categories by means of which we try to understand a book. A value judgment is a poor substitute for what cannot be translated into words about a book.

A great book of the past comes to us completely transformed from what it was originally. The critics and the literary historians have changed it, through the course of history, into an unrecognizable object. The more a work is loved and respected, thanks to the attention that has been paid to it, the more it is threatened by the erosive brilliance and theories of criticism. It is especially in *L'Espace littéraire* that Blanchot develops his theory that literary history is a place of degradation where a work, which was originally an opening out onto the world of a secret, the blossoming of some inner experience, is translated into a specific communication. An object which originally had no sense or value or truth is forced, by the industry of the literary historian, to take on a meaning and an ethical value. Because of the accumulated layers of criticism, it is difficult today to read a work, to have the experience of a reading where a work will appear to us in its genesis, in its hollowness, its secrecy, when we can read it as something that is being composed.

The new critic has to become a first reader of a work, and sensitive to the original silence which inhabits every work. The constant threat of criticism is the compulsive need of the critic to fill the silence of a work with words, words which Blanchot considers destructive. Even the critic approaches a work when it is already deformed by criticism. He has to try to see a work from the angle where it appears richest and truest: *rechercher le point où l'oeuvre est la plus grande, la plus vraie, la plus riche.*

In the book from which this quotation is taken, *Lautréamont et Sade,* Blanchot writes a criticism of criticism in order to justify his own method. He is not the first critic to point out the weakness of the traditional habit of ferreting out the sources of a work. As an example he uses *Les Chants de Maldoror* whose images some critics have traced to the Book of Revelation. But these images are also in Baudelaire. They are not literary reminiscences for Blanchot as much as they are examples of the merging in an artist's mind of collective myths and personal obsessions. Blanchot also criticizes the traditional habit of literary analysis which tends to isolate the commonplaces which form part of every literary work, and to exaggerate the truthfulness of a work.

The critic should not be so much concerned with the influence a work has, but with the initial movement or impulse that created the work, with the movement that literally formed the creator. The choice of *Les Chants de Maldoror* to illustrate this theory was wise indeed. It is one of those works, for which Maurice Blanchot has a marked predilection, that are creations of the self, where a

writer is born, where he returns to his origins. Lautréamont is one of a small group of writers to whom Blanchot
returns over and over again as authentic artists, whose
writing is a self-creation, whose writing contains a movement that comes only from themselves. Mallarmé occupies a high place in this group, and Hölderlin and Kafka
and René Char.

In his warnings against the misuse of literary sources
and thematic analysis, Blanchot has in mind the basic
concept he believes the critic should follow when he undertakes any writing about a work. It is the "essential
solitude" of a book (this phrase *la solitude essentielle*
occurs in *L'Espace littéraire*, p. 16). Every authentic literary creation (and Blanchot is interested solely in those
works he considers authentic) rises up from some kind of
need or demand which depends upon nothing outside of
itself. Blanchot never discusses a work in terms of its form,
in terms of its aesthetics. A work is not defined in terms of
its "classical" traits or "romantic" traits. A work is not
seen as something adhering to characteristics or rules of
some aesthetics. A work is always for Blanchot something
that makes itself and that thereby creates its author. This
man who wrote the book is a different personality from
the man who existed before the book was written. The
writing of a work creates another human being who is
impersonal and anonymous. He is separated from everyone, as the world of his novel or the world of his poem is a
solitude, a desert to which no one belongs. Art negates the
world as it creates its own world.

Thus Blanchot insists that the language of a book has
very little to do with the language we speak every day. A
work of art is something unreal, and artistic realism is a
conception deprived of meaning. These thoughts are in
the text of Blanchot's essay on Valéry's poetics, in *Faux
pas* (p. 150) where he writes: *l'oeuvre d'art est un irréel,*
and, at the end of the passage, *le réalisme artistique est
une conception privée de sens.*

It is therefore futile to judge a work in terms of its
relationship with reality, with life, with truthfulness. A

poem of Mallarmé or of Yeats cannot be discussed in the same way we discuss an event taking place in life. It has its own reality which is ambiguous and which resists any rational approach. Blanchot is here attacking the classical law of verisimilitude. The domain of a novel is always something outside of life. Blanchot derides the concept of realism so often applied to Balzac, and claims that the images and scenes of a Balzac novel have nothing to do with reality (see "L'Art du roman chez Balzac," in *Faux pas*, pp. 211–16).

With this concept of a work's essential solitude, Blanchot affirms his belief that a man when functioning as an artist is outside of the world. He does not even take the world as his starting point. A work of art is the absence of any relationship with the world. If the artist is a novelist, the language he uses is precisely the absence of the world, the absence of objects and beings. Blanchot sustains the thesis that the language of a writer is always the search for silence, because art is the negation of words spoken in real life. The absolute of literature is silence. The condition of literature is silence. Blanchot hereby denies the familiar concept of criticism that a book comes from other books.

Art, for Blanchot, is more related to death and to the void than it is related to life and plenitude. Words are destructive in the sense that they eradicate life. When a man succeeds in a literary creation, he disappears as a man, he quite literally annihilates himself. Thus Blanchot will not treat death as a theme in a literary work. Death is the work itself, the site of the work.

In *L'Espace littéraire*, in particular, Blanchot examines passages concerning the writer and death, in some of those authors for whom he has the greatest admiration: Kafka, Rilke, Gide, Sade, Proust, where each in his own way expresses a relationship between art and death. To put something in writing is equivalent to putting it under protection from death. Literary creation represents the same kind of freedom that death does. To create art is always the effort to reach an extreme which is never reached.

In this regard, the myth of Orpheus is revelatory for Blanchot. To write a poem and to die are equivalent or correspond to the same impulse. The instinct of Orpheus to descend to the underworld in order to find Eurydice is the impulse of the poet to create and therefore to seize death and to see death. But in terms of the myth, Orpheus is not allowed to look at the depths or at night or at his love. Night is revealed only when it is hidden in the work of the poet. It is as impossible for a man to look upon the subject of his poem as it is for him to die.

In his analysis of his myth of Orpheus, Blanchot comes as close as he ever does to a definition of art, or at least to a definition of the original source of all art. A truly inspired work has to bear a relationship with death. When art is merely the imitation of appearances in the world, it is realistic and uninspired. Inspiration (a word Blanchot reserves for authentic art) is the artist's contact with night or with the absence of the world. Such a theory explains Blanchot's deep sympathy with surrealism. As Oedipus once listened to the words of the oracle, so the modern surrealist learns to listen to the mysterious words of his subconscious.

The relationship of disciple would perhaps be too strong to designate that existing between Gaëtan Picon and Maurice Blanchot. But beyond any doubt, Blanchot has served as a model and as a guide for much of the very astute and penetrating criticism written by Picon. He too is a philosopher of literature, a new kind of critic determined to be unequivocally modern. He manifests no interest in what appears to be repetition and survival in contemporary literature. He is attracted by those signs of a new fermentation in today's culture and intrigued by those works of the past in as much as they seem to be foreshadowings and premonitions of the future. He favors the new and the unusual in literature and views with suspicions those values deemed permanent and traditional.

Picon's devotion to literature is as profound as that of Blanchot, and the criterion on which he bases his critical writing is very similar to Blanchot's: namely, the new relationship he is eager to discover between the vision of the writer and the expression into which the vision is translated. The art of the modern writer can no longer be defined with such a term as classical, because classical means fundamentally a vision of man that existed before any individual artist, and the realization of a literary form which can be learned by practice, by technique, by an adherence to rules. The other approach to literary creation, one which would be called "modern" by Picon, is that by which content and form are the same, by which the writer's vision and his expression are one and the same thing. In other words, a literary work is simultaneously an experience and a creation. The invention of a writer's style is everything. Flaubert had once expressed a belief in this concept when he said he would like to write a novel on nothing. And Stéphane Mallarmé, more than any other modern writer, systematized this belief. A mark of new criticism is the frequency with which Mallarmé is referred to by all the new critics in France, as the most modern of modern writers.

In the second volume of *Usage de la lecture*, Gaëtan Picon applies this theory to Balzac, in a hundred-page study entitled *Suite balzacienne*. He considers the transition between the early unsigned novels of Balzac and the masterpieces of *La Comédie humaine*, beginning with *Les Chouans*, not as the perfecting of a style or a technique. Rather it was the discovery of a "voice" which released the writer's vision. A book does not exist, even mentally, before it is written. A poem does not exist before one hears the music of the words. What was once called study and research in technique is today called the vision and the expression of the work. The classical position of the writer is one in which he appears submissive to the picture of a coherent universe. But the position of the modern writer, as defined by Picon, is that of the "demon" spirit, who in his creation, a Dionysian experience, rivals God as creator.

The difference between these two forms of writing, classical and modern, is perhaps to be found in the two ways of considering reality. The exterior world is real for the classicist, it is reasonable, it is matter governed by laws, and the words of the writer follow a discernible logic. The newer type of writer tends to look upon the world as a profuse and diffuse experience of vitality, as a disorder without reason, as jumbled as the polyvalence of images that flood his mind. Language, for the new writer, does not express what is real, it creates it. Language itself is reality.

As he describes (and praises) the art of Nathalie Sarraute, Picon's theory becomes quite clear. The story the novelist relates in *Le Planétarium*, for example, is not the gestures and the speech of the characters. Rather it is what takes place imperceptibly in the subconscious, in those fleeting nebulae of the subconscious that are constantly being transformed. Reality for Mme Sarraute is that world that precedes what is usually called reality. It is that world of agitation that precedes what we commonly call love or hate or jealousy.

Picon and Blanchot are critics fascinated by the mystery behind the birth of a book. Their criticism raises questions and proposes reflections on that mystery. The mystery is not so much the work itself, the completed work, as the attempt and the ambition it represents to create a work. *The Book to Come* (*le Livre à venir*) is the title Blanchot gives to a collection of texts which had first appeared in *La Nouvelle revue française* under the title *Recherches*, and which indicates the scope of his work of a critic: the discovery of a future work in a work already published but which may be unsuccessful.

The case of Antonin Artaud is examined by Blanchot as an example of the principle whereby a work's value for the critic is in the promise it makes of a future work. At the age of twenty-seven, Artaud sent to Jacques Rivière, editor of *La Nouvelle revue française*, poems which were not judged publishable. A correspondence between Artaud and Rivière ensued which Rivière finally judged of such interest that the letters and the poems were published. The poems thus became publishable when accompanied by the story of their experience and their deficiencies. In this way, the poems became *un livre à venir*.

When Mallarmé calls his future work the project he hopes to accomplish (which he never did accomplish), "Le Livre," the Book destined to give the Orphic explanation of the earth (*l'explication orphique de la terre*), he announced exactly the kind of mystery associated with the literary creation that intrigues such critics as Blanchot and Picon. In this word "explanation," Blanchot believes the poet means the development of man and the world by the art and the means of poetry. Poetry inaugurates an essential change in the universe, it initiates something new.

The type of question which concerns what might be called an abortive literature is one characteristic of the new generation of critics, men who fix their attention on the formal aspects of literature and who, in raising fundamental questions about critical method, have instigated, both knowingly and innocently, quarrels and polemical discussions. In defining his method, an individual critic seems often to be writing a manifesto, a program that is exclusive and that expressly indicates differences with other methods and tries even to invalidate other methods.

For example, the next two critics whose work will be examined, Georges Poulet and Jean-Pierre Richard, have opposed quite frankly much that is in the criticism of Maurice Blanchot. They claim their method of criticism derives from Marcel Raymond and Albert Béguin, with the support of such philosophers as Gaston Bachelard, Jean Wahl, and Jean-Paul Sartre. Without always specifying their differences, Poulet and Richard imply that their method or their approach to literature is incompatible with traditional academic criticism, with philological and historical explanations, with the work of such critics as Etiemble and Jean Paulhan, with Marxist writers, and with critics who emphasize the history of ideas.

In recent years, when the term "new critic" began being applied to writers of the generation of Poulet and Richard and to the next generation of critics, men in their thirties and forties, the critical assumptions and methods uniting such writers invited comparisons with the new critics who flourished in America in the mid-1930's. The so-called movement of "new criticism" was founded by four southern writers: John Crowe Ransom, the elder of the four and the leading spokesman, Allen Tate, Cleanth Brooks, and Robert Penn Warren. These four men were professors when engaged in defining their critical method, and in fact taught their method in their classrooms as well as introducing it in their published writings. Two critics from the north, R. P. Blackmur and Kenneth Burke, became associated very early with the southern critics. In addition to being critics, three of these men were poets: Ransom, Tate, and Blackmur; and Robert Penn Warren was a poet also and became a leading novelist. Edmund Wilson, the best known and most universally admired American critic of the twentieth century, is not usually associated with the group of new critics because of his insistence on historical and psychological data in his criticism.

In evaluating this American criticism, Paul de Man, in an excellent article published in *Critique*, uses with great felicity the term "formalistic" to describe the method of the new critics. The influence of the new criticism, first on American education, and then on American letters, cannot be exaggerated. This influence is probably stronger in America than the influence of the new French critics on French letters. In fact, the influence of the new French criticism today is probably stronger in America than it is in France. Whereas the French mind tends to react against a dogmatic approach to literary exegesis, the American mind, especially the university student, is anxious to find one method that can be learned and used, and one that holds out, in no unequivocal terms, the unique method of literary understanding. The extensive body of American critical writing is practically unknown in

France. The books of the new critics have not been translated into French, and neither has the history of the movement by Stanley Edgar Hyman (*The Armed Vision*) nor the writings of those American critics who oppose, to some degree at least, the principles of the new critics: Harry Levin in particular, Lionel Trilling, and Karl Shapiro.

The two movements of literary criticism in America and France took place at different moments, and the latter, in France, without any obvious influence from the former. And yet as the new French criticism has developed a formalistic approach to literary study, it often resembles the "new criticism" in its powers of exegesis and in the insufficiencies with historical and biographical methods it has pointed out.

The articles of faith held in common by the American and the French critics, and which often derive, knowingly or unknowingly, from *Principles of Literary Criticism* by the English linguist and psychologist, I. A. Richards, are related to a justification for art. This justification would define art as being the preservation of certain moments in the lives of exceptional individuals who have succeeded in narrating and controlling their experiences. The critic starts with this work and has to move in the direction opposite to that taken by the writer. He starts with the formal art and has to move back of that to the experience that produced the form. A close and sympathetic reading of a given text will offer the reader experiences sufficiently comparable to those that existed for the artist at the origins of his work. But the new French critics will claim that a work does not necessarily reflect an experience. The work of art is the experience itself. The critic's problem is not so much the reconstitution of a given experience which existed prior to the form of the art, as it is the examination of the means by which a work constitutes a whole, constitutes a world in itself.

The position of Georges Poulet is high among the new critics, and his influence is pervasive. In his writing, he emphasizes the degree to which the critic is a reader, an exceptional kind of reader who is able not only to move deeply within a book, to read all the works created by a given writer, but he is especially the reader able to enter another man's conscience, to identify himself with a process of thinking that is different from his own. In turn, the reader of an essay of Poulet isolates himself from the world, and is absorbed in the conscience and the consciousness of the writer who is the subject matter of the essay.

By method, and even perhaps by temperament, Poulet is quite close to Marcel Raymond about whom he has written an important essay in *Saggi e ricerche di letteratura francese* (1963). The reader-critic embarks upon an almost religious self-renunciation in order to become the receptacle of another presence. He must reach a state of total disinterestedness when an absence of egoism will permit him to welcome the work that is being read and studied. Any impulse to use this work for self-glorification must be annulled. In his will to identify himself with the mind of the writer he is studying, Poulet differs from the other new critics of his generation, and from Maurice Blanchot in particular.

The critic's goal for Georges Poulet is an awareness of the writer's awareness. *Une prise de conscience de la conscience* is a phrase he uses in the essay on Marcel Raymond, and by which he defines the limits of criticism. The reader first has to assimilate the meaning of the words he reads and then he is able to invade the conscience of the writer. Poulet believes that all the works of a writer form a unity and that by a process of dialectics he can perceive the interrelationships that form this unity. Dialectics is a way of presenting the complexities of a work. It is an approach from many different angles to the work in question.

Poulet frequently writes a second essay on his favorite authors in order to approach them from different sides and by different means: Baudelaire, Rousseau, Pascal, Balzac, Proust. And yet in each of these studies the critic looks upon all the works of the writer as forming one completed whole. The same passages are often used by Poulet to approach the work of a writer in a different manner, but always to point out that one given theme depends on all the themes, that any single passage of one book can be seen to reflect all the books of a writer. Poulet looks upon each book of a writer as joining with and reflecting his entire work, but also destroying at the same time the rigors of structure. A literary work is far too protean to be purely objective and characterized by a clearly outlined structure.

The language of the critic is a ceaseless effort to reach this identification with the conscience of a writer, a struggle to assimilate it and bring about some closeness between the writer's language and the critic's. The critic ends by prolonging the thought of the writer, because he has to appropriate terms and stylistic effects used by the writer. The critic learns to live on the life of the writer. And yet the critic's writing is never an empty echoing of the novelist or the poet. It is a deepening of the original work, a contemplation of the entire expanse of the work, and precisely that kind of contemplation which the writer himself never enjoyed.

But in this act of contemplation, Poulet is never apart from the work. His method is an ever-closer embracing of the work, as his language is an increasingly detailed ordering and elucidation of the work. When fully concentrated on one aspect of a work, Poulet analyzes an extraordinary number of subtle distinctions, at the end of which, themes or zones of the work which at first had been unclear or even invisible come into strong focus. He rarely concentrates his attention on an obvious element in the work, such as an image, but tends rather to choose prevalent sentiments or thoughts, and then proceeds to divide them into very precise nuances. These nuances are never seen as separate or isolated. Poulet demonstrates how one derives from the others, and how all of them are strictly interrelated.

In *Études sur le temps humain*, his first work, Poulet studied the individual conscience of a writer as it is revealed in all of his works. In *Les Métamorphoses du cercle,* one of his most recent books, he bases his reflections on the belief that the conscience of a historical period is unified and one, and is therefore similar to the unity of an individual conscience. This concept marks a new development in Poulet's criticism whereby the collective conscience of an age (the Renaissance, the Baroque period, the eighteenth century, romanticism) may be understood in the same way that an individual conscience is understood.

In addition to many magazine essays, Jean Starobinski has published three important books of criticism: *Montesquieu par lui-même* (1953), *Jean-Jacques Rousseau: La Transparence et l'obstacle* (1958) and *L'Oeil vivant* (1961). In his twentieth year, at the time of the Second World War, he wrote of the strange experience of feeling an inner peace, while fully aware that a war was raging outside. Georges Poulet, who has written an analysis of Starobinski's criticism, interprets this thought of the young Starobinski as an indication of the initial "situation" of the critic's thought when he realized the distance separating him from a universe on which his fate depended. It is Kafka's situation, namely a trial going on in a place to which he does not have access. It is the picture of man's solitude, of his conscience in exile. A penetrating awareness of self is equivalent to an awareness of being outside of the world.

In his more recent study of man seen as a being suffering from melancholy (*La Mélancolie de l'anatomiste, Tel quel,* Summer 1962), Jean Starobinski analyzes this experience of being excluded. The critic is the man miraculously endowed for understanding himself, but who gives himself over to the task of understanding something outside of himself. This is his function, this is his urgency. He must move in the direction of an object totally different from his own thought. He must seek to establish a relationship, an almost inconceivable relationship, with something not himself, with something foreign to himself. The critic appears, then, on one side, and the world, on the other side. What kind of relationship can be established between the two? To will such a relationship implies both pride and humility.

Starobinski has a predilection for the term "transparency." A man's mind and the world have to become transparent one to the other. By "world" is meant the world of Mallarmé or Montesquieu or Rousseau, the world of a writer that opens up to the inquiring mind of the critic. Each of these writers has for the critic Starobinski his own kind of transparency, of limpidity and clarity. For Mallarmé, for example, it is the poet's impersonality. For Montesquieu, it is the philosopher's desire to be clairvoyant. The critic attempts to discover the dream, the chimera, the obsession of the writer he is studying.

Starobinski's study of Rousseau is based upon the theme of transparency. Rousseau exemplifies a mind for whom the exterior world becomes identical with the mind. In such a world there is no difference between being and appearing. This kind of relationship or identification occurs in dreams where a man's being enters his thoughts and where his thoughts enter his being. It is the dream of transparency where a man's destiny becomes visible. The myth of man's destiny becomes the same as this myth of transparency or visibility.

In his essay on Mallarmé (*Mallarmé et la tradition poétique française*), Starobinski studies the phenomenon of preciosity by which the simple direct vulgar work designating an object is changed into a metaphor. An object is thereby spiritualized and made accessible to a man's intelligence, to his thought. A real object becomes an ideal object and thereby the man creating it (Mallarmé) and the reader of the poem no longer feels excluded from the world. Preciosity is thus seen to be one means by which the world and a man's thought become identical. Other critics, Maritain for example, have called this process the sin of angelism.

To reach this state of transparency is the exercise of man's freedom. The opposite of transparency is opaqueness which is the "obstacle" referred to in the subtitle of Starobinski's book on Rousseau. In each of his essays, Starobinski seems to be pursuing this dialogue between transparency and opaqueness, between the flexibility and spontaneity of the writer's mind, of the subject's mind, and the resistance to the spontaneity which is in the obstacles created by objects. The critic's study thus resembles the ancient debate between the mind and the body. Is there always something impenetrable to the mind? Is man's failure always his collision with matter?

L'Oeil vivant is a series of essays by Starobinski on Corneille, Racine, Rousseau, and Stendhal, which are studies of the writer's vision. The phenomenon of sight (*le regard*) is not only the capacity to see the world, to see an object, and to see through an object; it is also the discovery of the limitations of man's sight, the discovery that there is a point beyond which he cannot see. In other words, the act of seeing is the acceptance of a state of blindness. In his book on Rousseau, Starobinski has written: *Il faut vivre dans l'opacité* (p. 10). But from this inevitable succession of vision and blindness, Starobinski draws lessons for his art of criticism. If the world were totally crystalline, totally transparent, nothing could be distinguished or distinguishable. There would be no opposition by means of which what is illuminated can be distinguished from what is obscured. One can be blinded by total light, as one can be blinded by total darkness. The spirit of man is felt when it comes into contact with an obstacle.

Starobinski's alliance with the authors he admires, Montesquieu, Montaigne, Claudel, is a noble illustration of his critical method. His search, his investigation tends to annihilate the space between himself and the writer, and to create an interpenetration, a reciprocal movement of mental intimacy. Criticism is thus the means of making beings and thoughts penetrable.

The term "thematic criticism" has been used to describe the writing of several new critics, but especially that of

Jean-Pierre Richard. The study of the themes of a writer is one of the oldest forms of literary criticism. It was prevalent in the nineteenth century and even in the eighteenth, when the theme of honor in Corneille and the theme of passion in Racine were pursued in the investigation of critic after critic, and continue to be given as dissertation topics to schoolchildren. *La critique thématique* in the twentieth century, especially in the last two decades, differs from the term *la critique des thèmes* in stressing the fact that the theme of honor in Corneille's tragedies, for example, does not exclude other themes, in fact, many other themes.

Such a critic as Jean-Pierre Richard has trained himself to ask questions about a literary work that the author of the work did not ask himself. The theme of clemency was obviously in the mind of Corneille when he wrote *Cinna*, but the new critic will not focus more on clemency in *Cinna* than on other virtues and vices that make of the human heart a universe involving everything. "Thematic" is a newer word than "theme," and it is used precisely by the new critic, by a Richard for example, to indicate that there are themes in a literary work of whose meaning he is not absolutely sure, about which he has no absolute knowledge. The critic does not even know whether the author himself was troubled by the meaning of a given theme, or even aware that he was ignorant of its meaning. The new critic will go as far as to say that such ignorance on his part, and on the part of his author, is preferable to absolute knowledge.

"Thematic criticism," in this sense, is fully applicable to most of the new critics: to Bachelard in his analysis of fire and water, to Poulet in his analysis of the circle, to Starobinski in his analysis of the "eye" of Rousseau. But the rudimentary word "theme" would not be applicable to the multiple connotations and subtleties in such words as "fire," "circle," and "eye."

In his first two books, *Poésie et profondeur*, and *Littérature et sensation*, J.-P. Richard had quite literally studied one theme as it occurs in the writings of an author. Not

until *L'Univers imaginaire de Mallarmé* did he study all
the themes of a given writer. Critics of the nineteenth
century had, of course, studied an array of themes in
Balzac and Stendhal. When Richard studies swans, hair,
tombs, fans, etc. in Mallarmé, how does his criticism differ
from that of the earlier critics?

In the first place, the themes of a poet, and especially of
such a poet as Mallarmé, are more difficult to name than
the themes in a Balzac novel where there is so much social
and historical documentation. We do not have the proper
setting (historical or social) with which to understand
with any assurance the theme of a Mallarmé poem. "The
imaginary universe" of Richard's title would have been
called in an earlier period, quite simply, "The poetics" of
Mallarmé. Poetics, in its broadest meaning, is the way by
which a writer expresses his vision of the world. The
themes of a poet are not categorized by the voice of the
poet and therefore they have no interpretation before the
voice speaks in the poem.

When Richard analyzes the theme of light in Mallarmé, of sunlight on a windowpane, of lamps and candles,
he speaks of it as a phenomenon giving coherence to the
poet's universe, and never as the poetics of a literary
school or movement. He tries to avoid elevating themes
into myths. Rather than calling upon the myth of death
and transfiguration in Mallarmé, Richard uses such a term
as dualism, as the dualistic obsession of the poet (*obsession dualiste*).

The theme of death and transfiguration is everywhere in
Mallarmé's work, but Richard explains it as a cyclical
movement that is characteristic of the poet's creation. In
his close study of Mallarmé's project for a poem on the
death of his son Anatole (a manuscript published by the
critic as his *thèse complémentaire*), Richard reaches important conclusions about the function of poetry as evoca-
tion. If poetry is evocative, it therefore demands absence
and death and a sense of the past.

In Richard's most recent book, *Paysage de Chateaubriand* (1967), he undertakes to demonstrate the mechan-

ics of a writer in order to reveal secrets of which the writer himself was not conscious. One of the major functions of the new criticism is to force some of the great writers of the past, about whom we had come to believe that everything that could be known was known (Racine, Montesquieu, Chateaubriand, Mallarmé), to make new confessions about themselves. This is all the more extraordinary in Chateaubriand who had written so much about himself.

Richard studies the famous descriptions of landscapes in Chateaubriand, and tracks them down to the initial sensations and images wherein the writer betrays himself. The real landscape of Chateaubriand, for Richard, is not the scenes in Brittany and America, nor those in Greece and Rome and Jerusalem. In all of those scenes, Chateaubriand was held by signs of the void, by rivers and ruins that revealed the passing of time. All of his work is, in reality, for the critic, the setting of absence: *la mise-en-scène de l'absence.* The real landscape Chateaubriand was always describing was that of his soul, the inner landscape, that hollowness and emptiness, by which Chateaubriand was defining himself in relationship to the world. Richard interprets the vast work as a self-portrait. Combourg, the Parthenon, the Holy Sepulchre were only mirrors. The critic points out the resemblance between the two words: *miroirs* and *mémoires.*

Jean Rousset's book *Forme et signification* (1962) bears as subtitle: *Essais sur les structures littéraires de Corneille à Claudel.* The word *structure* is here deliberately used, and the book is a fine example of this rejuvenated criticism which seeks to explain a work by a methodical analysis of its structure and style.

Rousset has acknowledged his allegiance to Bachelard, Marcel Raymond, and Georges Poulet. He feels an affinity with Jean Starobinski, Jean-Pierre Richard, and Gaëtan Picon. The metaphors he uses in his critical writing are taken from the plastic arts: *formes, structures.* He is intent upon finding the meaning of a work in its style rather than in the human experience related in the book: the vision, the suffering, the thought. A work has its own life. It has its own intention, which is different from the intention of which the writer was conscious. This intention of the work is more important than the intention of the writer. A good example of this emphasis is in the chapter on *Madame Bovary* where Rousset studies the importance of windows in the novel and *la vue plongeante* from the windows.

This formalistic tendency of the new critics is in opposition to the idealism of traditional criticism. In its drastic reaction to the work of the older critic, it avoids, to its own peril perhaps, any discussion of the moral texture of the great literary works of the past. In his chapter on *Polyeucte,* Jean Rousset analyzes the tendril-like composition of Corneille's tragedy. He calls it *la composition en vrille* or *en boucle* of *Polyeucte.* It would be interesting to compare these pages of Rousset with the pages Péguy devoted to Corneille when he analyzed at great length the old familiar terms of *honneur* and *amour,* and with them defined the genius of the playwright.

Jean Rousset attracted considerable attention with his early book, *La Littérature de l'âge baroque en France: Circé et le Paon,* published in 1954. He has remained more rigorously "formalistic" than most of the new critics. Each of his seven essays in *Forme et signification* is a demonstration of what he calls the inner form of a work. Art comes from something real, but the art-form itself abolishes the real and substitutes for it a new reality. This new reality is the union of the writer's mind with a construction. Rousset claims that the emotions we feel in watching a tragedy are not the same as those we feel in our ordinary existence. Form in art creates its own meaning and engenders its own emotions. This word "form" does not signify for Rousset simple or complex proportions arranged in some harmonious sequence. Form is found in sets of relationships, in recurring patterns, in networks of orderings. There are centers of relationships in a work, designs that have to be found by the reader. Between the creator and the reader stands the critic who brings about an interchange between the two. In his role of intercessor or mediator, the critic knows that his intercession is never absolute, that he never possesses the work or understands it in any absolute sense. Rousset is discoverer of forms and designs in the works he studies.

In his introduction to *Forme et signification* Rousset undertakes to elucidate the methodology of his criticism. This text and Richard's introduction to his *L'Univers imaginaire de Mallarmé* are the most lucid explanations to date of the structuralist method in literary criticism.

It is a commonplace to repeat today that form and content are the same, that language and meaning are one. The new critics, Picon and Rousset perhaps more clearly than the others, keep reminding their readers that art in the nineteenth century and earlier was generally looked upon as the expression of some previous human experience. To move from some human experience to its creation in art would be simply a question of technique, a question of finding the means whereby the writer can recast, recapitulate the experience. This definition is no longer valid for the new critic. A literary work is no longer the expression of something, it is a creation. It shows something that was never seen previously. In a word, the new critics believe they have discovered a new understanding of art.

The critic's attention has to be focused on this enigmatic origin of a work as a structure. A work of art is not something created in nature, with a relationship to the real world, because it is created by the imagination of the artist. The free imagination of the artist is the only subject of his art. This is why such words as "separation" and "exile" return so frequently on the pages of Rousset. Art is a universe in itself that is added to the universe. A book is an absence. It is something about nothing. Flaubert longed to write a book about nothing: *un livre sur rien.* Such a project has obsessed the minds of many creative artists.

"Structures" are for Rousset those formal patterns (at times he calls them *liaisons*) that betray the universe of the mind and that are invented and reinvented by the artist whenever he needs them.

9

Structuralism:
From Barthes to Lévi-Strauss

The literary quarrel between Roland Barthes and Raymond Picard threw into relief some of the problems concerning literary criticism, and almost drew up into two camps those for and against the new criticism.

The source of the quarrel was the publication, in August 1963, of Barthes' book *Sur Racine*. The *avant-propose* of this volume and its last chapter, "Histoire ou littérature," are significant statements of a special attitude toward literature and criticism that is to count heavily in the various phases of the quarrel.

Fundamentally, for Roland Barthes, literary history does not exist, and criticism is impossible. What is called literary history is a series of critical monographs which no more constitutes the history of literature than a series of biographies of great Frenchmen would constitute a history of France. A real history of literature would be a study of the literary institution and would be founded on sociology and not on psychology. Literature would be studied in relation to the intellectual, social, and economic milieu in which it developed, and especially in relation to the idea that each period in history has of literature. This ideal program of literary history would hardly be contested by anyone today.

But—and herein lies the crux of the problem—the only important act that is of any importance for the critic is the creative literary act, the poem, the novel, the play, which is totally independent of that social, intellectual, and economic milieu that should be the subject matter of literary history. Whenever a critic uses history or biography or correspondence or any other document that resembles a "key" to a text, he has abandoned the study of the literary text in question. Energetically and with great precision, Barthes in the introduction and conclusion of his book revives and elaborates the thesis of Marcel Proust against the method of Sainte-Beuve (*Contre Sainte-Beuve*).

The basis for this attack is the belief that a literary work is a system of meanings that cannot be explained or deciphered in any objective manner. A literary work in its secretiveness might be compared to a door that opens only from the inside. If a critic attempts to open this door from the outside, he is duty-bound to acknowledge that it is with his own key.

In *Sur Racine* Barthes does have a key for his understanding of Racine, and this key is partly structuralist and partly psychoanalytical. He proposes to study the kind of character created by Racine—the *homo racinianus*—as an ethnologist would study a member of some primitive tribe. He announces that he will study this character without any reference to the life of Racine or to the historical period when Racine lived. On two occasions at least in the book he does not keep this promise. But on the whole, he does rely solely on the text of the eleven tragedies of Racine, on the habits and behavior of the characters in these plays.

Briefly stated, the thesis of Barthes, which is original and highly provocative and is substantiated with elaborate arguments and numerous quotations, claims that there is an absence of love and psychology in the plays of Racine. Such a thesis goes counter, of course, to a long-established and almost sacrosanct understanding of Racinian tragedy. For Barthes, the principal drive in Racine is not love, but a relationship based on coveteousness, a relationship based on authority. He finds in particular two kinds of relationships: one based on a long communal past, such as that of Bérénice and Antiochus (in *Bérénice*), and another kind which is a sudden violent revelation, such as that between Néron and Junie (in *Britannicus*). Barthes argues that sexuality does not count in these relationships as much as authority. In this kind of situation, the man may be forced into a feminine role (Hippolyte in *Phèdre*) or woman into a masculine role (Agrippine in *Britannicus* and Athalie in *Athalie*). The goal of the dramatic action is not the sexual possession of the one loved, but the defect or the destruction of the one loved. At the end of the action, the conqueror can see the defeat of the other. Sight is the possessive organ of man, according to Barthes.

This critic reduces all the conflicts in Racine to one conflict: that between father and son. Either the son kills the father, or the father kills the son. The highest moment in a Racine play is the discovery by the child that his father is evil, and that, despite this fact, he wishes to remain the child. The sons of Noah turned their eyes away from their father's nakedness, but they still remained his sons. This is the very brilliant passage of Barthes' discussion when he does call upon history and biography, by explaining this father-son role in the tragedies by Racine's life, by his desire to embrace the role of father and the role of king. Racine was divided in his affection for his king, Louis XIV, and his father, the priests of Port-Royal. This is a magnificent use of biography in literary criticism, although Barthes theoretically is opposed to such a device.

The major attack against *Sur Racine* and the critical method of Barthes is in a publication by the Sorbonne professor Raymond Picard, *Nouvelle critique ou nouvelle imposture?* The attack is more generally on Barthes' method than specifically on his new interpretation of Racine. It goes back to what Picard believes to have been Barthes' assault on academic criticism (*la critique universitaire*) where he reproves the exaggerated use of a biographical method bent upon establishing resemblances betweeen the life and the writings of an author, resemblances that are useful in explaining a work. It is the habit of explaining Oreste (in *Andromaque*) by Racine at the age of twenty-six, or Néron (in *Britannicus*) by Racine's lack of gratitude. (It is to be noticed that Barthes himself draws upon this analogy when he writes: *On sait l'importance de l'ingratitude dans la vie de Racine.*)

Racine has become the scapegoat for all the existing methods of criticism: for the scholarly and historically-orientated criticism of Raymond Picard, for the psycho-criticism of Charles Mauron, for the neo-Marxist criticism of Lucien Goldmann, and for the linguistic-structuralist criticism of Roland Barthes.

Picard and many of his university colleagues accuse the new critics of lacking solidity and any real value in the domain of explanation, of *explication de texte*. Barthes insists that objectivity is inconceivable in criticism. Therefore the critic is simply obligated to announce the type of subjective criticism he is using. This would mean, for Picard, that a critic can say anything about Racine, and even express himself dogmatically, and claim that what he says about one tragedy applies to all the tragedies. Picard cites the example of a critic defining tragic action in Racine by the relationship between sunlight and darkness, and claims that this relationship does not exist in *Bérénice* or *Iphigénie*.

In his very specific function of teacher, Picard denounces the effect of the dogmatic form of Barthes' criticism on students. They paraphrase him, use his terminology, and cease to read carefully the text they are trying to explain. (A similar phenomenon was observed in the middle sixties in America, where university students used, without understanding its limitations, the critical method of Northrop Frye.)

Picard believes that a text has objective elements, the first of which is the language itself. In approaching a text, the first duty of the reader-critic is to understand the meaning the words had for the writer. Then Picard believes a text should be integrated within the current of thought from which it came. The art of Racine, for example, is the result of a very specific moment in French civilization. These two steps, these two approaches to a text, are neglected by the new critics, according to Picard. He claims that they use literary texts, not for the pleasure of understanding them and experiencing them, but for the construction of a philosophy, or for a psychoanalytical study. This would be in keeping with their belief that a work is the product of the subconscious of the artist. The new critic, he says, is more interested in what preceded the literary creation than in the work itself.

In his answers to Picard's accusations, Roland Barthes has always insisted that Picard has inflated the whole matter, has exaggerated the difference, and especially the effects, and has refused to view the situation in terms of ideas and methods. He believes that Picard looks upon Racine as his property, and was displeased that a poacher had intruded on the estate. Barthes chose Racine because he is the most widely read and studied writer in French schools, and the supreme representative of the French national genius. Racine is therefore covered with taboos that Barthes considered it appropriate and timely to examine and eradicate.

Barthes defends his sentence about Racine's ingratitude by claiming that ingratitude is a widespread trait of character, whereas "Oreste is Racine at twenty-six" is a vapid assertion that would be denied by psychologists. When Barthes speaks of the "solarity" of Racine, he is using the language of his day and calling upon a structural-psychoanalytical analysis in the cultural meaning of the term. He would say that Picard has a perfect right not to accept such an analysis.

Whereas Picard insists there is no such thing as a clearly definable academic criticism (*critique universitaire*), Barthes says that there is, in the sense that the university is an institution with its language and style and scale of values that are controlled by the tradition of examinations. There is, he says, a university way of speaking about literature. He points out that Picard himself, in his preface to the Pléiade edition of Racine, attacks this *critique universitaire*. Barthes reserves the right to criticize the university and its methods. It is not a sanctified institution.

Barthes establishes an important distinction between scholarly and new criticism when he points out that the university studies the relationship existing between the avowed intentions of the writer and the work, the degree to which he succeeded in accomplishing what he set out to accomplish. The new critic is more intent on studying the relationship between a work of the past and a reader today. The life of a literary work is measured by the degree to which it appears different from the intention of the writer. In this definition Barthes has in mind a sentence of Valéry (one of the favorite writers of Picard): *L'oeuvre dure en tant qu'elle est capable de paraître tout autre que son auteur l'avait faite.*

Here, Barthes revindicates his position and that of the other new critics as lovers of literature, as the real guardians of the national heritage, because he, and they, are concerned with the problem of how to read Racine today, of how to read any of the classics. Barthes takes sides with university students today who are weary of a certain traditional vocabulary in criticism and platitudinous thought concerning literature. Society is constantly inventing and using a new language, and criticism should follow this example. Barthes would agree that his own special vocabulary will not survive very long.

Essais critiques, appearing in 1964, was Roland Barthes' fifth book. During the preceding ten years he had published: *Le Degré zéro de l'écriture* (1953), *Michelet par lui-même* (1954), *Mythologies* (1957), and *Sur Racine* (1963). The *Essais critiques* are articles and prefaces representing a vast range of reflections on literature: Voltaire, Baudelaire, Queneau, Robbe-Grillet, the new novel, structuralist criticism, the theatre of Brecht. They are sketches or studies of some of the newest intellectual discoveries in France: the sociology of Lévi-Strauss, the music of Boulez, the psychoanalysis of Lacan. The book is a faithful record of Barthes' evolving interests and preoccupations. He notes how we are leaving today the period of "committed literature." At one time, when he was studying Brecht's theatre, he had believed in the doctrine of commitment, especially in the theatre, but now he tends to believe that there is a whole part of literature that is condemned to having no effect on society, that will not be accepted by society.

His major interest, as a thinker and critic, is the discovery of how men give meaning to what is about them, and the meaning they give to literature. In the preface to *Essais critiques*, Barthes makes an attempt to define his critical method and activity. This definition is continued in the small volume *Critique et vérité* (1966), where he answers Picard's book *Nouvelle critique ou nouvelle imposture?* and other attacks made on the new criticism.

During the first half of the book (forty pages) Barthes takes up his own defense and launches out on a very decided assault on the critical method he dislikes. Many journalists have given support to the libelous attacks of Picard (in some of the most firmly established newspapers: *La Croix, Le Figaro, Le Monde*) and have attempted to exclude the new critics from the commitments. Barthes lists the harshest terms used in this rite of exclusion, in this execution: *crever, assassiner, pilori, échafaud*. In his turn, he castigates the older criticism as representing a shameful regression and compares it to capitalism. Traditional criticism expects a critic to speak of a book with objectivity and good taste and clarity. Barthes claims that such terms do not belong to our time: *goût* and *clarté* come from the seventeenth century; and *objectivité* comes from positivism of the nineteenth century.

In the second half of the book Barthes undertakes to explain the meaning, the method, and the purpose of the new criticism. All distinctions between literary genres have disappeared. What is left is what he calls *une écriture*. In this regard he quotes an important sentence in the avant-propos of J.-M. Le Clézio's *La Fièvre*. The critic is no longer merely the handmaid or the valet of the creative artist. His commentary involves other disciplines — philosophy and the human sciences — as soon as the symbolic nature of language is admitted. As soon as the pluralistic nature of speech is accepted, the way is opened up to dreams, allusions, symbolism. The critics pass from philosophy to linguistics, from a literal commentary to semantics. Reading means touching the text with one's eyes. But out of that act grows the desire to write. The literary adventure is contained in these two verbs: *lire* and *écrire*. In places, the arguments of Barthes are extremely difficult to follow, especially in the passage where he discusses the triple crown of language: science, criticism, reading (*science, critique, lecture*).

In the history of criticism *Critique et vérité*, a succinct and yet richly documented argument, is a declaration of rights of man as critic. The questions it raises are: What is a literary work? What is the meaning of a work? It questions the relationship between man today and art, between man and the reading he does, and between man and his own thinking. A book is first a summation of signs and symbols. Then it is the meaning we give to the signs. And third, it is our reading of the book, our desire to identify ourselves with it and to put something of ourselves in it. Criticism is neither purely objective nor purely subjective for Barthes. It is a drama taking place between an objective content and a subjectivity (the reader's) trying to penetrate the content.

Today as we read Pascal, Racine, and Mallarmé, we should not omit from our reading the new knowledge that has come to us from sociology, psychoanalysis, Marxism, and the human sciences. When the critic Barthes speaks to us today about Racine, he is throwing light upon Racine, upon Roland Barthes, and upon us the readers.

The fullest and most lucid treatment of the Picard-Barthes controversy was written by Serge Doubrovski in 1966: *Pourquoi la nouvelle critique?* This critic, who teaches French literature in the United States, analyzes and criticizes those he considers the major critical systems today: those of Barthes, of Lucien Goldmann, and of Jean-Paul Sartre. Unhesitatingly Doubrovski is on the side of Barthes, and yet he criticizes Barthes for not remaining faithful to the existentialist philosophy of Kierkegaard, Jaspers, Heidegger, Marcel, and Sartre.

The book that originally instigated the quarrel, *Sur Racine* by Barthes, has been replaced by generalities representing two critical methods. If Racine can be explained in terms of a certain number of biographical, psychological, and aesthetic conventions, can't he also be explained by another set of conventions which would be sociological and psychoanalytical? On page 246 of *Essais critiques* Barthes establishes a list of those critics who with himself represent a method of literary interpretation that is opposed to the positivistic method inherited from Gustave Lanson. The names he lists are: Sartre, Bachelard, Goldmann, Poulet, Starobinski, Jean-Paul Weber, René Girard, J.-P. Richard. The novelty of their criticism is perhaps not quite as novel as they claim. It remains clearly within the humanistic explanation of literature which also is the tradition of Sainte-Beuve and the university tradition of Lanson. The new criticism explores the hidden meanings and intentions of a work, and it is mistaken only when it insists that this is the only possible kind of research. On this point at least, Picard seems to be justified.

Barthes is not as psychocritical as Mauron, for example. His conception of criticism is closer to the study of linguistics and the structural anthropology of Lévi-Strauss. A literary work is first the object of language before it is the result of psychological and social conditions. In the same way that a painting is first a canvas and colored paint before it is a nude or a still life.

The controversy goes far beyond the immediate hostility between Barthes and Picard. In its deepest implications, it is the ancient opposition between two kinds of mind: the authoritarian mind which on the whole characterizes Picard, and the more open, the more critical mind engaged in research and exploration which is that of Barthes. It is a new version of the old quarrel between the ancients and the moderns, between the law and heresy. For the new critics, literature is something autonomous. It is not a means but an end. It is not an adornment or a mirror. It is independent. There is no one canonical meaning to a work. A symbol in literature signifies a plurality of meanings. The critic in the new sense given by Barthes is the man who first falls in love with the language of a work, and then falls in love with his own language as it develops in contact with the work. This concept of love indicates that there is not only beauty in the work, but desire for the work in the heart of the critic.

In two books in particular, *Le Dieu caché* (1956), and *Pour une sociologie du roman* (1964), Lucien Goldmann proposes a method of literary criticism which he calls *structuraliste-génétique*, and which develops one aspect of the new criticism, one that strives to build interpretation on a scientific basis. Goldmann is violently opposed to what he calls "ingenious and subjective speculations" about literary works. He believes that today scientific thinking has progressed far enough to allow a critic to understand and explain human relationships as they appear in a literary work. This, of course, was the hope and the belief also of Sainte-Beuve, of Taine, and of Renan in the second half of the nineteenth century.

The kind of writer whom Goldmann will qualify with the term "genius" is one who has a world vision (*une vision du monde*). He represents the aspirations, the ideas, and the sentiments of a social group (which is usually a social class). The genius offers in his work the maximum social consciousness, and thereby establishes an equation between the vision of the world as seen by a group and the world created in a work of literature. In *Le Dieu caché* Goldmann analyses the tragic vision of the world of Pascal and Racine.

The social group is the real creator of this vision. The *Pensées* of Pascal and the tragedies of Racine are ways or processes for the understanding of the tragic vision of the world. The structure of a literary work has to be seen in its relationship with the structure of the social group. The structure of the tragic conscience in the seventeenth century corresponds to the structure of the Jansenist group. The Jansenist conscience is a condemnation of a world that is basically evil. It is a conscience that has no hope of changing the world.

The method of Goldmann is a synthesis of the present-day human sciences and the Marxist tradition. His criticism is a sociological explanation. The more purely literary criticism must be subordinated to sociological criticism, in the same way that philosophy was looked upon as the handmaid of theology in the Middle Ages. Since for Lucien Goldmann a literary work is the expression given to a vision of the world, the first indispensable study of the critic is that vision, and such a study is, of course, purely sociological. In other words, sociology has the same function in Goldmann's criticism that psychoanalysis has in Mauron's. Goldmann's contribution to criticism has been the revelation of essential meanings in Pascal and Racine, and in the novels of Malraux and Robbe-Grillet, that have been neglected or omitted in research before him. More firmly than any other critic today he forces his reader to consider and to see the relationship existing between the writer and society.

In the middle 1960's, Claude Lévi-Strauss occupied in French thought the place that Sartre had occupied between 1945 and 1955. He is an anthropologist who holds the chair of social anthropology at the Collège de France, and whose ideas, reaching far beyond his anthropological research, have deeply affected the development of literary criticism. The term "structuralism" is closely associated with this scientist. Almost all of his books have been translated into English. He has become, in the last few years, an international figure.

Whereas traditional anthropology looks upon the human mind as evolving through the millennia in much the same way that man evolved physically, Lévi-Strauss contends that the human mind has been in full possession of its powers and patterns since the first instances of human society. He is changing the meaning given to such terms as "savage" and "civilized" cultures.

Claude Lévi-Strauss was born in Brussels in 1908 and grew up in France. He studied philosophy because he found every other branch of learning detestable. In 1935 he went to Brazil to teach at the University of São Paulo, and began there, in Brazilian jungles, his anthropological field trips.

The key to his method is the principle that reality is that which is hidden. Even in the study of sociology, it is not enough simply to observe in order to see, nor to see in order to understand. Social phenomena are phenomena in the Greek sense of manifestations and appearances. Behind these manifestations the scientist must try to discover a structure, an organizing scheme of a logical-mathematical order. If order exists anywhere—say in the behavior of the atom—then it exists everywhere, in the brain of man at every moment in his history.

Every history, according to Lévi-Strauss, obeys abstract laws of thought which are often hidden from the conscious attentiveness of individuals who apply them subconsciously. The sociologist's task is to discover these laws. This kind of sociology represents therefore a form of Platonism. At one level man builds a social system to answer his needs. But at another level, far deeper, he is following a pattern existing in the human intellect that shapes all these things that social man uses. Everything seems divided between the sentiment of necessity for social structures and the sentiment of the gratuitousness in social structures. As in a text of a Villon poem, we read both an obvious exterior meaning and gradually decode, gradually decipher an inner secret meaning.

Linguists and structural anthropologists believe that human speech and human society originated at the same time. But speech is only one way for society to explain itself. Other ways, which Lévi-Strauss looks upon as languages as explicit as speech itself, are: literature, art, music, myths, religions, cooking, tatooing, commerce or barter.

The so-called arts of civilization already existed in the Stone Age: weaving, pottery, agriculture, the domestication of animals. Lévi-Strauss attacks the theory of human perfectibility by insisting that what man is today he was already in the past. Such a theory is an attack on modern

theories of history as defined by Marxism and existentialism. Sartre believes that man can learn a great deal from
history. He has always appeared indifferent to science. For
Lévi-Strauss history is not dependable. As he constructs
his science-oriented point of view, he tends to point out
what he considers a series of failures in the history of
civilized man: the failures of Christianity, of humanism,
of communism, of existentialism.

In the light of these failures, structuralism is a hope and
is thus being studied in advanced university seminars
throughout the world. Le nouveau roman as it developed
in France has a relationship with structuralism. Instead of
telling a story and analyzing a character, the novelist
studies the function of writing and calls upon his subconscious intellect rather than the classical rules of literary
composition. The formlessness of the new fiction is in
reality a reliance on inspiration of the subconscious. The
literary critics are now using structuralism to reexamine
and elevate the role of the critic. They claim, with considerable forcefulness as in the case of Roland Barthes,
that the aesthetic laws governing the writing of a novel or
a poem also govern the writing of criticism. Criticism is
inevitably criticism of the work in question and criticism
of the critic. Lévi-Strauss himself might not subscribe to
such theories, but his work is being used to justify them.

That aspect of the investigations carried out by Lévi-
Strauss which interests the critics the most is the process
of decoding a myth, of ferreting out the hidden meaning
of a myth. This means the deciphering of the filigraine of
history, of the motif that has been lost. That very motif
may turn out to be the principle by which a product of
the human mind is organized. In such an investigation
Lévi-Strauss starts with a fact rather than with an idea,
with a reality rather than with a philosophical system.

The first volume of his Mythologiques is called Le Cru
et le cuit (The Raw and the Cooked). Here he develops
his belief that the mind of man functions according to the
same laws and logic, whether it is Aristotle's mind or the

mind of a Brazilian Indian. The second volume of *Mytho-logiques* is called *Du Miel aux cendres* (*From Honey to Ashes*), in which the anthropologist moves away from cooking in order to consider honey which precedes cooking and tobacco which follows cooking. *Le cru* was used to signify "nature," and *le cuit*, "culture." *Le miel* and *le tabac* are more dynamic. "Honey" corresponds to a descent toward nature, and "tobacco" indicates a rising toward the supernatural. In analyzing the thinking of a savage, *le cru* and *le cuit* reveal qualities: What is rotted and fresh, what is slow and swift. Whereas *le miel* and *le tabac* reveal the logic of forms: the empty and the full, the container and the contained, the internal and the external, the included and the excluded.

Lévi-Strauss has been accused of separating research from that of other sciences. He claims this is a false accusation and points out that his ethnological research has utilized the findings of history, geography, and social customs. In the same way, he believes the quarrel between new critics and traditional critics ill-founded. Structuralism is, for him, a powerful means of investigation, but it should not sacrifice investigations carried out in a more traditional manner.

The principal quarrel involving Lévi-Strauss is over his conception of history. For Jean-Paul Sartre, history is carried out by an actor we call "man." He believes that man has the power and the duty to move beyond social structures. The important matter for Sartre is not what has been done to man, but what he has done to what has been done to him. (*L'essentiel n'est pas ce que l'on fait de l'homme mais ce qu'il fait de ce qu'on a fait de lui.*) Claude Lévi-Strauss answers Sartre by saying that man seen as the actor of history is an ethnological fact related only to a certain type of society—our own. He explains Sartre's seeming irritation with him as a fear that philosophy is being evicted by the tremendous expansion of human sciences and the development of contemporary scientific thought. Yet he points out that Sartre has written some excellent structuralist analyses and that a recent issue of *Les Temps modernes*, Sartre's magazine, devoted to structuralism, is a just representation of the method.

In a special issue of *L'Arc*, Sartre groups under the heading of "structuralists" the names of Lévi-Strauss, Foucault, Althusser, and Jacques Lacan. At the end of 1966 the Editions du Seuil published the *Écrits* of Dr. Lacan, a nine-hundred-page book comprising articles written between 1936 and 1966 and printed in magazines which are now very difficult to find. These articles are all on the science of the psyche, and represent, in the clinical research they relate, a return to Freud. They are a new attempt to study the coherence and organization in the work of the Viennese doctor, an attempt to apply to the subconscious those precise laws described by Lévi-Strauss in *La Pensée sauvage*.

Écrits is made up of the case studies and the experiences of a psychoanalyst. They are seminar papers given first before doctors at Sainte Anne where Lacan has taught for ten years. Such men as Georges Bataille and Merleau-Ponty had often urged Lacan to publish these communications. The book, almost more than any other, has drawn up into two opposing ranks the structuralists and the existentialists. This opposition, which exists almost in the form of polemics, is an absurdity for Lacan, for the simple reason that structuralism as a doctrine and a method has been gradually forming over a number of years. But those who tend to see clear-cut divergence of opinion everywhere place Sartre and his followers on one side, and on the other side a regiment of structuralists with four leaders: Lévi-Strauss as ethnologist, Althusser as Marxist, Michel Foucault as philosopher, and Lacan as psychoanalyst.

Lacan himself has pointed out major differences between his own interests and those of the other three men. Lévi-Strauss, for example, is not very much concerned with psychoanalysis. The Marxian research carried out by Althusser has no relationship with Lacan's work. Foucault does not draw upon the Freudian position.

Structuralism has been used to group these four men together, but it is more than probable that the word *structure* does not have exactly the same meaning for each one. Between Lacan and Sartre many differences are clear. In Sartre's philosophy, man (or the subject) and his conscience are indissolubly joined. In Freud's philosophy this bond is broken. The subconscious is not the same thing as the conscious, and the two are not usually joined. Sartre's objections are directed not against Lacan as much as against Freud. Sartre has never evinced any real interest in Freudian psychoanalysis. And yet in his writing, there are very fine analyses of those psychic parts of man that lie just below the conscious. There is, for example, in *L'Être et le néant*, a remarkable analysis of the phenomenology of sadistic passion. Yet for the scientist Jacques Lacan, such an analysis of Sartre is brilliant but not exact, and therefore not useful. A physician who has studied cases of sadism knows that nothing really takes place as it is described in Sartre's exposé. In other words, there is a difference between a philosopher and a clinical research scholar.

Lacan believes that neither he nor Lévi-Strauss has the total disregard for history that Sartre accuses them of having. History has to be studied to provide an adequate background for the training of psychoanalysts. They need also more linguistic discipline, more knowledge of the history of religions and myths, and indoctrination in the new mathematics. If this kind of program is ever carried out, Lacan believes that psychoanalysis will become what it should be: a science.

In the domain of French thought and criticism, between 1950 and 1965, something comparable to a reversal of values has taken place that seems to parallel the new movements in literature, in the novel and the theatre in particular. Sartre is already being looked upon as the last metaphysician. A new generation of scholars has come after him who use a different vocabulary. "Anthropology" has replaced "philosophy," for example. The word "system" has taken the place of "subject" or "conscience." "Structure" is used now instead of "history." One of Sartre's favorite words, "praxis," has been abandoned for "language." There is little unanimity of opinion among the new masters and the new disciples. Despite the ever-growing influence of Lévi-Strauss, Lacan, Althusser, and Foucault, Jean-Paul Sartre is still today, in 1967, the strongest and the most popular expression of French thought.

He is not hostile to structuralism provided its exponents remain aware of the limitation of its method. Sartre has pointed out that Lévi-Strauss himself has warned against the abusive use and application of structuralism, especially in the domain of literary criticism. A structuralist analysis is valuable, for example, in revealing the significance of myths in primitive societies. The function of a myth is, according to Sartre, the integration of disagreeable elements that threaten the life of a society. But every society, even the most primitive, has a history which cannot be reduced to an internal process, an internal order. This order is a structure for Lévi-Strauss. But history, for Sartre, is disorder. History is constantly undoing the order of society.

In the light of structuralism, Sartre has redefined what he believes to be the function of philosophy. It represents the effort of totalized man (*homme totalisé*) to understand the meaning of totalization (*totalisation*). History is for Sartre a movement of perpetual totalization. No science can replace this, because each science applies to one domain of man's life. Whereas the scientific method is analytical, philosophy is dialectical. It is an investigation about man, who is the totalizing (*totaliseur*) subject of history.

Sartre defines structures as everything that has been done to man. They are the subject matter of the human sciences. What man does is history, namely the effort to exceed, to go beyond the structures. Philosophy is the meeting point (*la charnière*) between structures and history. For Sartre, Marxism is the one method that takes into consideration the ensemble of history. It is not a fixed system. It is a project to be accomplished. He believes that Marxism today has refused to integrate new knowledge concerning man, and has thus become impoverished. The question today is, according to Sartre, whether Marxism will be allowed to die or whether it will be given new life.

Only on the surface, today in 1967, does literature remain literary and science scientific and history bloody. Under the surface there is another sense of reality that is forming in the research and the writings of a certain number of intellectuals who are modifying our concepts of sociology, psychology, linguistics, and the history of our civilization. A hundred years from now, our age may be characterized not by the conquest of space and technical progress, but by the development of a certain number of theories that have altered our concept of man and civilization: the biological spiritualism of Teilhard de Chardin, for example, and the structuralist sociology of Lévi-Strauss. Michel Foucault's book of 1966, *Les Mots et les choses*, will have its place in this domain of ideas, which exceeds the limitations of literature but which is related to problems of the new criticism.

The announced subject of the book is the relationship between man and language, from the sixteenth century to today. The method employed by Foucault is similar to that of Claude Lévi-Strauss in his book *Tristes tropiques* where the anthropologist analyzes a form of thought or civilization by describing its mental structure without comparing it to any other mental structure. Whereas Dürkheim and the first sociologists looked upon primitive tribes as inferior to us, as representing lower levels of human development because, for example, they did not have a generic word for "water," but a series of words designating rainwater, ocean water, drinking water, etc., Lévi-Strauss has taught that it is futile to impose our own language and mentality on primitive peoples, and that they should not be looked upon as savages or mentally deficient. Michel Foucault has applied this method and this principle to his study of the language of Europeans during four centuries and has pointed out many possible errors in the so-called humanist tradition. Our ancestors of the Renaissance or of the age of Voltaire are not social units forming a part of a long chain that ends with us, with our reasonableness and our scepticism. Each society of the European past was a closed world having its own logic that is not our logic. The myths of humanism and progress are undermined by Foucault's study.

Soon after the First World War, Paul Valéry reminded Europeans, in a now famous essay, that civilizations are mortal. Michel Foucault is saying in his book of 1966 that civilizations are discontinuous and that a civilization depends upon its language. Each age is independent and has its own instruments, its own methods for understanding. Each age differs from all others arbitrarily and not through any evolutionary process. For example, Foucault says that today French civilization is not one that comes at the end of a long Christian, rationalistic, humanistic tradition which started with the essays of Montaigne in the sixteenth century and ended with the death of Gide in 1951. The French of 1966 are not the heirs of Montaigne, of Racine, of Voltaire, and of Victor Hugo. Each of the ages in French history, represented by a major writer, has its own autonomy, its own mentality, its own structure, its own language. They followed one another in chronological sequence but owed very little to one another. Each one was a world by itself. France of today is still another world.

The subtitle of *Les Mots et les choses* is *Une archéologie des sciences humaines*. The word "archeology" is important for Foucault, because the study of the past, the literary study, for example, of Montaigne and Voltaire, is archeology. It is not, for him, the study of ideas and forms that we today live on and can assimilate. In other words, French literature is a field for excavation. We read Voltaire as if we are looking at a museum piece. This is certainly the attitude of countless students being introduced to the literature of the past in our secondary schools and universities. It might be said that many students in French lycées reach the conclusions of Michel Foucault without having recourse to his book.

This emphasis on the lack on continuity from one century to another results in a deflating of the white man's superiority. We have no ancestors on whom to rely. But the critics of a critic are always swift in rising up, and already some of the first readers of Foucault's book are insisting that there are traces of continuity in French civilization, traces of the influence of Aristotle from century to century, of Latin syntax which has disciplined the thought and the logic of the French sentence from the sixteenth century through the nineteenth century. It might be difficult for Foucault to deny the perpetuity of certain notions, such as Christian charity, divine love, and romantic love in age after age of French civilization.

Sartre, in discussing Foucault's presentation calls it a "geology," a series of layers, of geological strata of French soil. He asks how thought can rise up from such conditions. To explain the emergence of thought, Sartre says that Foucault would have to call upon *praxis* or history. History is for Sartre continuity and movement, and not a succession of immobilities as it appears to be in the explanation of *Les Mots et les choses*. Sartre explains the success of Foucault's book by saying that it represents an eclectic synthesis in which the art of the "new novel," structuralism, linguistics, Lacan's psychoanalysis, and *Tel quel* are utilized one after the other, in order to demonstrate the impossibility of history.

Les Mots et les choses is Michel Foucault's fourth book (when it was published in 1966, he was thirty-eight years old), and it is a more elaborate and more meaningful enterprise than the earlier books on Raymond Roussel, on the history of insanity (*Histoire de la folie*), and on the history of man's notions about sickness (*La Naissance de la clinique: Une archéologie du regard médical*). The new book is an effort to demonstrate that the nature of man we observe today, which is the basis of our philosophy called humanism, is an invention of recent times. "Man is not the oldest problem," Foucault writes, "nor the most constant problem with which human knowledge is concerned."

In the history of knowledge, man is merely a moment, a brief appearance (Foucault uses the words *un pli*), destined to disappear. Foucault wants to point out the fragility of any understanding of man, whether Christian or Marxist. Although he gives evidence of filial respect for Merleau-Ponty and Sartre, Foucault's book tends to relegate all the manifestations of existentialist thought to a museum. He undertakes to answer such questions as: What manner of thinking characterizes our period, our culture, and our society? What is the *système* (a key word for Foucault) that directs scientific investigation today and the reactions of man's sensitivity?

10

Conclusion:
Crisis in Our Age of Criticism

During the past one hundred years, the century that began with Sainte-Beuve and ends with the so-called "structural-ists" today, the image of the literary critic has undergone considerable change. What this image has become was however latent in Sainte-Beuve. In fact, what we under-stand today by literary criticism is largely the product of the nineteenth century. Before that time, criticism was a branch of rhetoric, and the critic resembled a certain type of schoolmaster who pointed out the beauties of a text that he felt his readers should know about, and, in the negative sense, pointed out all departures from the rules that the text illustrated. Before Sainte-Beuve, the French critic was the guardian of rules and the defender of good taste.

With the example of Sainte-Beuve, the critic became a writer, and literary criticism became an art of writing. Today the distinction that was made in the past between literary criticism and literary creation is somewhat out-dated. In France, it was largely Sainte-Beuve who helped to bring this about and convince his audience that criti-cism is a particular art of literature. Since the writings of Baudelaire, one hundred years ago, the critic has grown into the stature of a writer and an artist who expresses himself fully and deeply. Behind a piece of critical writing, and even behind an individual judgment in that piece, it is possible to sense the whole of the critic's personality and the whole of his experience as a man.

During the course of the twentieth century

especially—this was already evident in the latter part of the nineteenth century—critical writing and imaginative writing developed in similar ways and in close contact one with the other. Both the critic and the novelist came to rely more and more on such sciences as sociology, psychology, and semantics. It was Sainte-Beuve who first explained that the knowledge of the critic has to extend far beyond our knowledge of the text, that his knowledge has to include theology and philosophy as well as psychology and sociology. The critic has to know not only the work in question but the man who wrote the work, his habits of life, his family, his friends, the environment in which he lived, and the climate and the history of the age in which he lived. This preoccupation went so far in Sainte-Beuve, that is, went so far away from the text itself, that many writers today claim he is not a literary critic at all. It is true that he is looked upon today more as a great European writer (when one thinks of his impressive *Port-Royal*) than as a critic. But he emphasized the belief that criticism must be creative, and he was largely responsible for criticism being recognized as an art, as a branch of literature. His role was all important in the preparation of what is called today "the age of criticism," and even, more specifically, in the creation of what is called "the new criticism."

In the middle of the nineteenth century, Sainte-Beuve foresaw, as a few years later Walter Pater foresaw, the change that was to come for the critic. They were among the last of the cultivated critics who lived easily in contact with the past and were able to keep abreast of all the important publications of their day. But soon after their time the amount of publications that should concern the critic became overwhelming and has continued to grow more and more oppressively overwhelming. The type of Renaissance man who had time and leisure to know a good deal about every important subject of his day is no longer possible in our day.

Little wonder that by the end of the century and the beginning of the twentieth a new type of critic emerged who relied on the range of his own interests and on the depth and perceptiveness of his own impressions. Every critic is impressionistic to some extent, but extreme cases of impressionist criticism gave the category a bad connotation. This kind of critic was looked upon as a dilettante. It was inevitable that the next type of critic to succeed Sainte-Beuve and the impressionist was the specialist.

The type of critic-writer, not the specialist, whose work is creative as well as critical, and whose criticism is an important aspect of his ideal, namely the depiction of the whole man, is nobly illustrated in the nineteenth century, in England with Coleridge, in Germany with Goethe, in France with Baudelaire. In the twentieth century, despite the very marked trend toward specialization, this type of critic-writer continued, more notably in France than in other countries, in the work of Péguy, Gide, Proust, Valéry, Sartre.

Taine in his critical method was far more dogmatic than Sainte-Beuve, and he appears today as the innovator of the specialist type of critic, of the critic intent on making criticism a science. Taine expounded his belief that when a critic discovered "the race, the moment, and the milieu" of a writer he could predict with certainty the type of book this man would write. This was far more narrowly scientific in scope than the method of Sainte-Beuve, and ultimately it stressed not values inherent in the work itself, but information concerning the writer and concerning the society in which he lived.

This so-called "scientism" of Taine is apparent today, to some degree at least, in psychoanalytical criticism and in Marxist criticism. These are scientific forms in the sense that they are based on a determinist philosophy: a psychoanalyst critic studies the implications in words and images that often reveal obsessions and complexes of the writer; and a Marxist critic studies the social function of art. The French critics of these schools tend to be more professional than others, but their professionalism never prevents them from pointing out the danger of systems. During the last two decades when a vast amount of profes-

sional criticism has been published in France, there has
been at the same time considerable criticism of the criticism, which serves as control and check and discipline.

Whenever the scientific in criticism, as in Taine and in
the structuralists today, risks becoming too overbearing,
some kind of corrective is cited. French critics, even the
most highly specialized and the most rigorously scientific,
do not neglect the admonitions, the advice, and the perceptive views of a Baudelaire, a Gide, and a Valéry. One
sentence of Baudelaire, written when he was twenty-five in
his *Salon de 1846*, in answer to the question, "What good
is criticism?" stands even today as a creed for critics:
"Criticism must be partial, passionate, political, that is to
say, written from an exclusive point of view, but from the
point of view that opens up the widest horizon." Each
word of the definition has its wisdom, and the total
thought seems capable of embracing more than one school
of criticism.

"Partial" criticism would seem to indicate that an individual is speaking, one who possesses his own convictions
and his own approach to the subject. "Passionate" is the
second term, and one particularly believed in by Baudelaire. It means a full commitment of sympathy and feeling
on the part of the critic. In other words, criticism must
not be a cold dispassionate exercise. "Political," the third
adjective, has the overtones of combative writing, of a
willingness to wager all on one side, to take a strong
position and hold it. The kind of criticism Baudelaire has
in mind must be "written from an exclusive point of
view," which means from a viewpoint strong enough to be
a philosophy, or a system that coordinates all the activities
of man, that sees a unifying force in all of his experiences,
that permits him to place literature in a scheme of human
values. Here the critic is called upon to be a thinker, to be
almost a philosopher, to be at least learned and wise.

The conclusion of Baudelaire's sentence is the most
striking part of the definition. All the other clearly stated
parts of the definition head up to this conclusion. Criticism in its highest instances must be that kind that "opens

up the widest horizon." The literary critic is essentially the reader of literature whose perceptions and knowledge are largely formed by that discipline. But his critical principles may, and usually do, have a basis in some other discipline or body of knowledge: theology, for example, or philosophy, politics or science or some branch of the human sciences. The danger will always be for the critic to rely too heavily on his religious convictions, or on his political commitments, or on his scientific knowledge. This danger has been pointed out especially by the Canadian critic Northrop Frye. Baudelaire seems to be saying that in order to reach a final critical judgment the critic has to respond first in a vibrant and personal way to the text he is reading. Then he has to analyze his reactions in terms of his philosophy of man and his understanding of the world.

It would be disastrous for a critic to apply dogmatically his religious belief or his political conviction to a work of art and distort his aesthetic perception. This would mean that a Catholic would do an injustice to Milton, and an agnostic would bungle his explanation of Dante. Northrop Frye takes too absolute a view when he says that critical principles must not be contaminated by such matters as the critic's own philosophy or politics. T. S. Eliot held a viewpoint closer to Baudelaire's: "Literary criticism," he wrote, "should be completed by criticism from a definite ethical and theological standpoint." A critic's perceptions and knowledge, after all, have been sharpened by his personal convictions and his personal philosophy. Jacques Maritain as a critic cannot eradicate his knowledge of Thomism. T. S. Eliot as a critic inevitably remains close to Anglicanism. Tolstoy has a strong moralistic bias. Sartre remains an existentialist philosopher when he writes of Genet and Flaubert. Goldmann does not renounce his Marxist philosophy when he writes of Racine and Pascal.

In almost every reader, learned or illiterate, criticism is a natural and inevitable reaction. It is comparable to blushing at a moment of emotion, and to a gesticulation at a moment of surprise. The first form of criticism is the reader's immediate reaction to a book: admiration or reservation or a refusal to accept the book. When the actual criticism is written down, the critic attempts to solidify and deepen this initial reaction, and often, during the course of the writing, he rectifies the first impression and even transforms it totally.

Today's formal literary criticism has become something quite different from this type of judgment, the thoughtful reflective explanation of enjoyment or dislike which traditional criticism represented. Criticism in its new ambition is a means of knowing man or understanding something about him. The subtlety and even profundity of the best contemporary criticism are its most striking characteristics. The development, in the sense of change that has taken place in criticism, is far more drastic than any development visible in other forms of writing today. Baudelaire and Rimbaud would not be overly startled if they read the poetry of René Char or Henri Michaux or Saint-John Perse. But it is more than likely that Sainte-Beuve would be bewildered if he read Barthes or Starobinski or Blanchot.

The great proliferation of critical writing in France, and in other countries as well, since the Second World War is a historical fact and one that is not always easy to explain. It seems to have developed and spread at the expense of first-rate creative writing. It may be the consequence of the development of the human sciences of which the new criticism often appears to be a specific application. Whereas earlier criticism involved a rudimentary knowledge of psychology and sociology, structuralist criticism today is based on anthropology enriched by psychoanalysis, the phenomenology of perception, Marxism, and our present-day knowledge of the history of man and the history of societies.

It is impossible for criticism, in any of its forms, not to have a moral meaning. This is because the ultimate objective of criticism, no matter how impressionistic or how scientific it may be, is to provide man with a better understanding of himself. Criticism is an intelligible communication between man and other men, between reader and author, and even between the author and that part of himself he had not clearly understood.

Even if the critic cannot obliterate his personal philosophy, the best state of mind for him to be in when he attempts to penetrate the private world of a writer is an attitude as free as possible, as emptied as possible of all preconceived notions. We expect a critic to be receptive and attentive in the highest degree, and this involves a self-renunciation, a determination to allow no personal doctrine, no personal sentiment to intervene between his mind and the book he is reading. It is of course impossible to reach or maintain such a state, and every critic and every reader of a critic know this. Even those critics who seem the most open and supple, the most detached from dogmatism, retain some of their most private predilections: Du Bos, for example, in his *Approximations,* Gide in his *Prétextes,* Mallarmé in his *Divagations,* Jacques Rivière in his *Études,* Valéry in his *Variétés.*

When all is said, it is perhaps preferable for a critic not to obscure his own vision of the world when he attempts to see and explain the vision of another writer. A literary work is a language, and therefore the means of carrying on a dialogue between a man's conscience and another conscience. There is perhaps a greater profit to be gathered by this dialogue we call criticism when the critic's mind is radically different from the temperament and the intellect of the writer as they are expressed in his book. Our understanding of Pascal's *Pensées* has only gained by the interpretations it has received from the agnostic Sainte-Beuve, from the Catholic priest Steinmann, and from the Marxist Lucien Goldmann.

When criticism is primarily apologetics or polemics, the critic has not sought to understand in order to explain. He has appropriated immediately his role of militant apostle. This happens as often with zealous Catholic critics as it does with intellectual Communists. A recent work of Roger Garaudy, *D'un réalisme sans rivages,* is an example of criticism by a Communist writer who never allows his philosophy to interfere with his aesthetic understanding and appreciation of the three subjects of his book: Picasso, Saint-John Perse, and Kafka. This is a model of criticism free from any polemical overtones. In the chapter on Picasso, Garaudy does not see in the paintings symptoms of bourgeois decadence. As a literary critic in his chapter on Saint-John Perse, he considers a work antithetical to communism and studies in it the poet's love of the world, his joy in naming the things of the world, and his confidence in man's ability to redress the wrongs of history.

For fifty years, in thirty-six books (without counting the numerous articles), Henri Massis was in France the frankly polemical critic. With unabated ardor he participated in all the political, literary, and moral *causes célèbres* of the twentieth century. He was the critic who extolled Barrès and who detested Gide whom he looked upon as Satan's emissary. He was drawn to Péguy, but believed strongly in the political views of Maurras. He was violently opposed to surrealism and yet he was unwilling not to give Cocteau a position in French letters. He treated Maritain as if he were a saint, and Valéry as if he were a monster of hyperintellectualism. Massis was a fighter, an *engagé*, who took a position and held it firmly and vocally, on such subjects as patriotism, the alexandrine line, the problems of the contemporary novel, and Marxism.

In a book published in 1967, at the age of eighty, *Au long d'une vie*, the long career of Massis as polemicist appears in a somewhat different light, where the belligerency of the critic's Catholic stand is softened into an intellectual adventure, into even a sentimental adventure. As he relives his life of a writer, the attacks and the offenses for which he was known are seen as experiences of love. The book is the history of the century, told from a critical moralistic viewpoint, that begins with Montmartre and even the rue Ravignan, famous because of Picasso and Apollinaire in the first decade, and that ends with meetings between Massis and Camus. These men, so opposed in many ways, were united in their belief in the young, in their efforts to propose something to young Frenchmen that might guide them and reassure them, as once Massis himself was inspired by his teacher Alain, and Camus by his teacher Jean Grenier.

The young do not write criticism in any literal sense, but they often enact the critical spirit in their demonstrations, in their histrionic arguments, in their revolt which in the following generation is often recast into literary criticism. Henri Massis, as a polemical writer between 1910 and 1940, was an irritant and a stimulant. In writing the history of his polemical activities in *Au long d'une vie*, he has become the historian of those moral perturbations that marked two generations of French culture. Today the "happenings," conducted by young people in Paris, are critical manifestoes that may well in time dictate forms of critical writing.

In the Théâtre de la Chimère on the rue Fontaine, in 1966, "happenings" were stopped by the Paris police. A few years earlier, French artists escaping to America revealed to young Americans such examples of revolt as dadaism, surrealism, futurism, abstract art, and *musique sérielle*. Inspired by the happenings in the United States, by the creations of John Cage, by the tableaux of Allan Kaprow, the French happenings began in 1960, under the instigation of Jean-Jacques Lebel, not in France, but in Venice. A Tinguely statue was thrown into the Grand Canal, and people, dressed in black, followed a funeral gondola. These spontaneous spectacles by nonprofessional actors have now many adepts in addition to Lebel. Ben, in Nice, is an important impresario and he has enlisted the interest of the young novelist of Nice, Jean-Marie Le Clézio. French interpreters look upon a happening, not so much as an example of pop art and a recent discovery of beatniks, as an offshoot of dadaism and Artaud's theatre of cruelty. It is not an artistic work as much as it is a form of criticism, a means of ridding man of his inhibitions and taboos. Psychiatrists are already using happenings as ways to bring about mental rehabilitation.

A very strong sense of "responsibility" appeared in the writings of French novelists in the 1930's and early 1940's, in the works notably of those major novelists who reached a wide reading public: Malraux, Bernanos, and Camus. These very novelists, in their critical writing, developed a new or renewed understanding of literature, a more human, a more flexible theory of art than the theories of Gide and Proust in the preceding generation. The basis for this new critical viewpoint was the general crisis that affected literature in the 1930's, when the writer began to feel how specifically "situated" he was in terms of his age, and how fundamentally responsible he was for his age, for its defeats and its ambitions. He ceased being concerned with man in his relationship with an outmoded form of humanism or with man in his relationship with bourgeois values. The novels of Malraux, Bernanos, and Camus are the first expressions of our contemporary anguish. In these books man's conscience is at times somewhat lucid, but for the most part it is baffled and confused. It is man's conscience beaten by, but still trying to understand, such hardbound absolutistic institutions as the bourgeoisie, and capitalism, and Christianity, as they developed in the nineteenth century.

Malraux in his theory of art, Bernanos in his denunciation of the bourgeois spirit, and Camus in his essay on Sisyphus are witnesses to a moment in the history of French criticism when it was impossible for a writer or a critic to look upon a work of art solely as a work of art, solely as an expression of beauty. They were the first, who came into their own as critics after the Second World War, to lay the basis of a philosophical criticism that claimed there is no one unique method for understanding and explaining a work of art. This critical stance has continued to count for most of the critics who have written since 1950, and even for the most rigidly formalistic of the structuralists. The most noteworthy mark of contemporary criticism is the desire to be the conscience of literature, to integrate and exceed all the most vital aspects of past critical methods.

The critic as judge, whose pronouncements appear absolute—a Boileau in the seventeenth century, a Voltaire in the eighteenth, a Julien Benda in the first part of the twentieth—is almost nonexistent in contemporary French culture. Traces of absolutism are still visible in definitions of method but not in aesthetic or moral judgments of a work, or in interpretations of a work. On the whole, the critic is now hostile to judgments. It is difficult for him to find in his age unassailable beliefs of a social or ideological nature that would authorize unassailable critical judgments.

In his critical observations, the writer today tends to combine erudition with intuition. A purely scientific or formalistic elucidation of a work is still considered by a few as useless, but it is incorporated by most critics into their writing, by an Etiemble who emphasizes erudition, and by a Barthes who emphasizes structural analysis. Whereas at one time in the history of criticism, Sainte-Beuve explained a work by everything that is not in the work, today the critic keeps his attention focused on the completed work.

Even the concept that criticism is an understanding of a given work is seriously doubted today. This is due to traditional ways of understanding literature: namely, by the reconstruction of the personality of the writer as it is projected by literary forms into a work, or by the reconstruction of a philosophy which pervades the work but not always in an obvious manner. Such investigations, carried out for the avowed purpose of understanding a work, would be considered by many of the new critics as a betrayal of the work itself.

Actually the new critics seem more bent on criticizing (and even judging) criticism than on criticizing a novel or a play. To do this, the critic has first to make up his mind about what the essence of the literary act is. This is a prime consideration for Blanchot and Poulet. They are more concerned with the mystery of words in general than with the mystery of a given text. During the last three years, most of the critical attention in France has been focused on a debate over method, and the criticism of texts has been neglected, or at least has seemed less compelling than the quarrel over method. The debate opposes two sides, two factors—literary criticism and literary history—and yet its significance is in the hope, the more or less implied hope, that the two sides can join and use one another. In all fairness it should be noted however that at times in the debate the two sides appear forever irreconcilable.

Is it possible to be specific about the basic difference between the two sides? One side would seem to believe that a work can be defined objectively, that there is a fixed meaning of a work. The basis of Roland Barthes' critical method is a denial of the objectivity of a work's meaning. He insists that language is at all times open to a multiplicity of meanings. A work continues to be read from century to century, precisely because it offers a succession of meanings which apply to the criteria of sense and sensibility of a given moment in history.

This polyvalence of meaning encouraged Georges Poulet to omit any reference to a historical viewpoint and to start with the reading of the work itself. Solely from this reading, he creates a new author, one he calls an *auteur mythique*. He never refers to the man himself, the historical figure who wrote the book, because Poulet believes that the writer is totally different from the man who bears his name. An author creates himself as he creates his work: *L'auteur se crée avec l'oeuvre*. Jean-Paul Sartre's study of Genet (*Saint Genet, comédien et martyr*) is the fullest and most brilliant illustration of this theory.

A novel, therefore, is the fictional self of the novelist (i.e., the subjective self of the writer) speaking to the subjectivity of the reader. Hence, the multiplicity of meanings of the work, and the difficulty for the critic to discover in this multiplicity anything but an inner coherence, an inner unity. Several of the new critics now believe that the critic needs to develop, not an analytical comprehension of the work he is studying, but a dialectical comprehension. Sartre himself has defined dialectical reason (*la raison dialectique*) as a power that goes beyond the search for a total meaning and one that is capable of organizing and surpassing analytical reason.

Such a thesis makes it clear that phenomenology is appropriating for itself more and more place in criticism. The danger of this appropriation is the possible harm it will do to literature. As criticism grows into a more and more recognized form of literature, it is substituting for literary language a philosophical jargon. The risk it is running at this moment, in the late 1960's, is to end up in a formalism as rigid as the formalism exemplified in Sainte-Beuve that it is determined to combat and destroy.

A noteworthy example of this danger and risk is in the new critical work of Sartre on Flaubert, of which one part appeared in *Les Temps modernes*, May 1966: *La Conscience de classe chez Flaubert*. For some time now Sartre has borne a grudge against Flaubert. In 1947, in *Qu'est-ce que la littérature?*, he denounced the novelist's attitude toward the Commune. In this new writing of 1966 Sartre continues to look upon Flaubert as the supreme type of bourgeois who never failed to affirm his allegiance to his class. Flaubert's famous hatred for the bourgeoisie which he declared so openly and so persistently throughout his career, was merely, for Sartre, an expression of his desire to be a bourgeois.

Sartre argues that Flaubert's resentment was the passive reaction of an unrecognized child. He felt excluded from his class, but he was also an accomplice to his class. He anathematized the bourgeoisie and at the same time reconstituted it in his own person by his own bourgeois practices. His role of an artist was the way by which he distinguished himself from the masses. However subtle this analysis of Flaubert's class consciousness is, it does not help very much in explaining his work. Other critics have in these same years brought valuable insights and recognition to the work of a man who has suffered from a partial eclipse since the war. Nathalie Sarraute has hailed Flaubert as being the real forerunner of the "new novel." Victor Brombert, has in a recent book written in English, *The Novels of Flaubert: A Study of Themes and Techniques,* included reference to biographical and social influences on Flaubert, in a study that is primarily concerned with the text.

At this moment in its evolution, French literary criticism has reached a phase that almost resembles a crisis. A similar crisis seems also to exist in American literary criticism. The two literatures share similar problems, methods and ambitions in the domain of criticism. American critics tend to know French criticism far better than the French know what is being published by American critics. However, this situation is beginning to change.

The word "crisis" is not too strong to use because of the danger, already felt by some of the most sensitive of the critics, of alliances. Literary criticism has joined to itself a large number of *sciences humaines*, which, while enriching it on the one hand, have tended to force it at times into almost unrecognizable complexities and obscurities. The more resolutely scientific of the structuralists, such as Claude Lévi-Strauss, are offering a promise to the literary critics that if they adhere to such a method as that being advocated by structural anthropology, literary criticism may one day be worthy of joining the ranks of *les sciences humaines*. But it must be recorded that such a promise does not appeal to all of the new critics.

In America, the effect of Jane Harrison's *Themis* (1912), of Maud Bodkin's *Archetypal Patterns in Poetry*, (1934), and of Northrup Frye's *Anatomy of Criticism*, (1957), has been to make out of the history, the analysis and the interpretation of myths, a form of literary criticism. The effect of Dürkheim, Bergson, Marie Bonaparte, Bachelard, and more recently of Lacan and Lévi-Strauss has been similar in French literary criticism.

In both countries, because of these rich alliances, the role of literature in human life has been enormously increased. One has come to expect from literature much more than ever before in its history. The danger is that one has come to expect from literature more than it contains in its pure art of literature, and that the ardor of the critic exceeds at times the results of his investigations.

Thanks to the critics in France and America, who have relied heavily on the development of anthropological studies from Dürkheim to Lévi-Strauss, and on the development of myth-interpretation from Jane Harrison through Bachelard and Northrop Frye, literature has come to be recognized not only as an art in itself, with its laws and themes and techniques, but as that force able to represent and even unify a society, as that force revealing the common nature of man. Such a claim is admirably analyzed in Maud Bodkin's first chapter of *Archetypal Patterns in Poetry*. Henri Bergson, writing at approximately the same time as Maud Bodkin, advanced a similar theory that art and literature are the guardians of society and function especially at that moment in history when society gives signs of disintegrating. The vitality and the persistence of myths in literature give to that art its communal basis, its power to preserve the patterns of society even when society is threatened. Geoffrey Hartman, with clear-sighted justice, has called Jane Harrison the first structuralist, who in *Themis*, as early as 1912, assembled a large amount of evidence concerning the ritual origin of art. The contribution of Gilbert Murray in *Themis*, a chapter entitled "Excursus on the Ritual Forms Preserved in Greek Tragedies," is an expansion of Aristotle's analysis of plot structure in tragedy, and has exerted a marked influence on American criticism, notably the writings of Northrop Frye.

The belief that society is based upon forms of myth and is instinctively reenacting the life-cycle of myth, is today in France a vital part of structuralism and hence of that literary criticism associated with structuralism. The expression of myth in literature is not always as overt as it is in *Ulysses* of James Joyce, in *Fragments du Narcisse* of Valéry, of *Les Chants de Maldoror* of Lautréamont. It is far more difficult to discover the mythical patterns in such works as *Partage de midi* of Claudel, or *Amers* of Saint-John Perse, or *En attendant Godot* of Samuel Beckett. Psychoanalysis with its techniques for bringing to light concealed meanings is a principal method for discovering the hidden or half-hidden myths in such works. Jung's theory of the collective unconscious, which contends that primitive patterns of life are recorded in the memory of

each man, has encouraged the adventurous critic to discover in a given work not only the story of the writer's
generation, but the story of earlier ages and cultures.
Because of the myths of mankind, a reader today can be
trained to identify himself with the past as easily as he
identifies himself with his own period. The modern critic
is propounding, albeit unconsciously at times, that the
cohesiveness of society, the unity of man, and the purpose
of man are best revealed by literature. Such an overwhelming claim goes very far in explaining why today—doubtless
momentarily—literary criticism has surpassed other literary forms in France and America.

In both traditions, English and French, the modern
critic has shown during the past thirty years a predilection
for studying the greatest writers, for returning to the past
both distant and immediate, and reconsidering those writers whose vision justifies such attention: Shakespeare and
Racine primarily, as the greatest dramatists since the
Greeks; Melville, Balzac, and Joyce as novelists who are
visionaries and re-creators of myths; Eliot, Rimbaud, and
Mallarmé whose art is of such complexity that it has to be
approached from several viewpoints—linguistics, etymology, mythology. The new critic pays no attention to
judging such matters as value or morality or beauty in the
work of these writers. He is concerned principally with
interpreting the vision as it appears throughout the entire
work of the artist: G. Wilson Knight on Shakespeare,
Roland Barthes on Racine, D. H. Lawrence on Melville,
Albert Béguin on Balzac, Harry Levin on Joyce, F. O.
Matthiessen on Eliot, Jacques Rivière on Rimbaud, Jean-
Pierre Richard on Mallarmé. Incidents and symbols are
examined as parts of a totality by these critics. They are
quite literally concerned with the parts and the totality of
a structure. In his art of interpretation, the critic's vision
has to match the artist's vision.

A ritualistic interpretation of literature is a way back to
the origins of literature. Francis Fergusson's chapter on
Hamlet in *The Idea of a Theatre* is an explicit and very
brilliant interpretation of the tragedy in terms of its ritual

origins. It illustrates moreover the continuity that exists in the succession of literary forms from one century to another. If life is the way to death, then literature can be looked upon as the way back to life.

Whereas the literary critic tends to use myths in his interpretation of an artist's vision, Lévi-Strauss uses them to resolve the oppositions, the antinomies in social life. For the anthropologist, myths are fundamentally conservative elements. They preserve those elements that are needed by society. Hercules reappears as Superman and Tarzan. Orpheus reappears in the Beatles and Bob Dylan.

There is nothing exclusively French about the theories of myth and ritual, as there is nothing exclusively French about structuralism. But structuralism, about 1962, succeeded to existentialism in France as a fashionable philosophy. French intellectuals tend to think in terms of movements and schools of thought. They tend especially to group around eminent figures. Claude Lévi-Strauss has, in this sense, replaced Jean-Paul Sartre. Although as yet, structuralism has had no effect on literature, it seems to be classified today as one of the sciences of man. It is at least a method of analysis. No one formula defines it with any accuracy, because it is concerned with so many different matters: the structures of languages, the structures of myths, the structures of the unconscious, structures of the plastic arts, musical structures, literary structures.

Never before in the history of literature have literary texts been so carefully scrutinized as they are today by critics who in the elaboration of their analysis call upon a number of disciplines and bodies of knowledge. The author of a text is one man, but his text has a multiplicity of different meanings because it attempts to give, by means of language, something that approaches the wealth of all human existence. There is a historical meaning to a text, a sociological meaning, a psychology behind the text, a meaning in the text that can only be reached through stylistics. Literary expression is a fusion of many things which have their sources in the multiple modes of existence and in the varied so-called disciplines of human knowledge. No one method in criticism, no one discipline in the series could possibly exhaust the meanings of a text.

There is general agreement today among most critics and students of literature that every book is a species of biography of the author; if not an autobiography, at least a spiritualized biography. This theory would apply to works as different as *La Chartreuse de Parme* of Stendhal, *Prose pour des Esseintes* of Mallarmé, and *L'Exil et le royaume* of Albert Camus. Therefore for the understanding of such works, it is logical and desirable to draw upon whatever illumination psychoanalysis can provide. This is, in fact, the basis of Charles Mauron's psychocriticism.

If the work being examined is a comedy or a tragedy, an ode or a sonnet, it is imperative to know the rules governing such a specific genre, and at least something about the origins and the development of the genre through the centuries. A sense of literary history is, in other words, indispensable to the literary critic, if he is analyzing such forms as *La Cantatrice chauve* of Ionesco, *Lorenzaccio* of Musset, *La Maison fermée* of Claudel, and *Semper eadem* of Baudelaire.

The study of linguistics, and the allied sciences of phonetics and etymology, are of great help to a critic who is trying to explain why the sound and the rhythm of a particular line in a poem of Apollinaire or in an alexandrine of Racine are able to exert a spell over the listener. Why is a listener held as much, or even more, by the pure sound of a line, by the succession of vowels and the rhythmical groupings of words, as he is by the meaning of the line? Leo Spitzer, in his analysis of *le récit de Théramène* in the fifth act of Racine's *Phèdre*, draws as much on the sound effects of the passage, as he does on the mythological allusions, and on the structure of the passage in its relationship to the entire tragedy.

Literature is based upon human facts, human activities. A major part of the critic's destiny is an understanding of these facts and these activities. And that is why the literary critic of 1967 is necessarily involved in the principal ideological currents of 1967: structuralism, existentialism, Freudian psychoanalysis, Jungian psychoanalysis, and

Marxism, as well as in such continuing disciplines as history, linguistics, and literary history.

It is obvious from such a listing that no one critic can reach a total criticism of a given work. If he is Lucien Goldmann, he will draw mainly on sociology and aesthetics. If he is Charles Mauron, he will draw mainly on psychoanalysis and aesthetics. Each one of the new critics is intent upon that kind of research that will unify in his criticism the largest number of significant meanings of a text.

In each century of French thought, there have been efforts, usually sporadic, to dethrone philosophy, to point out in particular the uselessness of "metaphysics." Pierre Bayle did this in the seventeenth century, Voltaire in the eighteenth, Auguste Comte in the nineteenth. In certain quarters today the word "metaphysics" is as outmoded as the word "mysticism." And yet, even if there is a physiological explanation for the forming of a thought in a man's brain, any attempt on the part of that man to articulate his relationship with the world, any effort to formulate a system by which he sees his individual being as a part of the existence of the world, is a form of metaphysics, whether he calls it that or not.

Several French critics, whose minds are alert and open to everything going on around them, who never fail to relate, when feasible, their critical writing to problems of the day, have consistently refused to ally themselves with any obvious philosophical position. Within this group, whose influence is very marked on the young, on those approaching literature critically for the first time, are critics associated with universities and whose careers are at least partly devoted to the direction of doctoral dissertations. In their professional objectivity, these critics have not aligned themselves with any ideology: Jean Pommier of the Collège de France, René Etiemble of the Sorbonne, and three French critics whose university careers have for the most part been spent in the United States: Henri Peyre of Yale, Germaine Brée of Wisconsin, and Jean Hytier of Columbia University.

The groups of critics already named are many and

diversified: thematic critics, such as Poulet, Richard, Starobinski; structuralists, such as Goldmann and Barthes;
psychoanalytical critics, such as Bachelard and Mauron;
university critics who remain disengaged from any school
of criticism and from any philosophical alliance. In spite
of their diversity of views and practices, they have one
belief in common: Literature is the richest discourse
which the human mind has created and addresses to other
human minds. The art of the critic is the power to animate
this discourse, to have it speak, to use every means
possible to bring it into the consciousness of men.

Whereas specific laws governing methods of criticism
differ from group to group, modern French criticism does
offer, in each major instance, the criticism of the totality
of a work, the painstaking clarification of all that is im-
plicit in a work. This is the natural, the inevitable point at
which criticism and philosophy join. What is called criticism in its simplest sense, and what is called philosophy in
its simplest sense, cannot avoid an involvement with the
ideology of the age in which they are written. The modern
critic's determination to consider and explain the total
work of a writer is in itself a philosophical tendency.
Criticism, like philosophy, always remains to be done. It
has endlessly to be done anew, after it undoes what has
already been done. The critic and the philosopher both
reincarnate the now familiar figure of Sisyphus and his
rock.

It would be difficult to find in the history of French
literature a period comparable to the half century that
begins with 1917, at the end of the First World War, and
terminates with the triumph of the structuralists and the
appearance in 1967 of such works as *Le Retour du tragique* by Jean-Marie Domenach and the first volume of
Paul Guth's *Histoire de la littérature française: Des origines épiques au siècle des lumières*. The changes in literature, the metamorphoses of form (to borrow Pierre de
Boisdeffre's title) that have taken place in that short

period of time, have stimulated the critics and challenged them to a careful scrutiny not only of the works themselves that demonstrate the metamorphoses but also their methods of explaining literature and the crises that Frenchmen and all other men are going through.

The period witnessed, first, the decline of forms that had become sterile (the plays, for example, of Rostand, Porto-Riche, and Henry Bataille), and then, the birth of new literary works embracing the moral and metaphysical preoccupations of our time. The writings of Gide, Proust, Malraux, Bernanos, Sartre show the writer as a man deliberately disengaging himself from dilettantism and immersing himself in history, in order to become involved with the ethical and political problems of his day. *La Condition humaine* of Malraux is perhaps by its title and content the most noteworthy example of this age in French history. But every great literature has advanced hypotheses on the value of man and on the meaning of his adventure in this world. Man's fate in this world fascinated Stendhal and Balzac as much as it does today André Malraux and Jean-Paul Sartre.

And yet there is a difference between the books in French literature of 1850 and those of 1950. The difference comes from the deeper and the more tragic crisis of man's fate, the crisis of Western humanism which the past fifty years have witnessed. The philosophical intention of the newer literary works is far more grave, far more tragic than French literature has ever known in its history. Nothing in the past is quite comparable to the philosophical intention of *Sodome et Gomorrhe* of Proust, of *Sous le soleil de Satan* of Bernanos, of *Moïra* of Julien Green, of *La Nausée* of Sartre, and of *Fin de partie* of Beckett.

On the whole, the French critic has had very little difficulty in analyzing the philosophical intentions of such modern works. But such a dramatic term as "metamorphosis" is even more applicable to another trait of the new literature, the tendency in every domain of art to devaluate the expression of man's lucid consciousness in order for the writer, and other types of artists as well, to fix his attention on the subconscious, on the instincts of man, and especially on his erotic instincts. This emphasis involves all manifestations of the irrational and the mystical and even the heroic. Here the work of the critic has certainly begun to be felt, in his preliminary efforts to understand this aspect of contemporary literature. But here the scope is so vast and intricate that it is obvious the critic has made a mere beginning.

Those clear regions of consciousness and power and glory, from which spoke such writers as Voltaire and Hugo and Zola, where moral and political situations were predominant, have been deserted, by Proust first, and then by a host of French writers, for regions where the mind of man lives in an atmosphere of uncertainty and anguish and humiliation, where his consciousness explores his most intimate feelings, where an invisible personality lives. The metamorphoses which twentieth-century literature did undergo, and which have been more profoundly explored by Maurice Blanchot than by any other critic, have been brought about by symbolism, surrealism, psychoanalysis, phenomenology, the development of abstract art, the influence of the movies, by the many experiments by which traditional art has been radically altered: the theatre of the absurd, the new novel, pop art, happenings. The task of the critic is arduous indeed when he attempts to explain the poetry of René Char, the novels of Jean Genet, the writings of Samuel Beckett.

The critical method of Bourget where a work is explained in terms of the writer's immersion in the problems and intellectual dramas of his age would hardly be adequate to explain these contemporary books. And even the newest methods of Barthes and Starobinski with their emphasis on structures and obsessional themes are too limited in providing illumination on the works they study. But they do illuminate the style of the writer, that unique way of speaking that the writer has found to correspond to what is most personal in his vision.

The new criticism which has analyzed so brilliantly the style of a writer as the real key to the writer's thought, will be followed by other methods of criticism in France.

Already, in such a book as Jean-Marie Domenach's *Le Retour du tragique*, the critic uses a literary work as a commentary on its age, as an interpretation of the dreams and defeats and obsessions, both conscious and unconscious, of a country and of a world. Once again in the history of French criticism, the word tragedy is invoked in order to illuminate our age with its myths, its hopes, and its despair.

It is a provocative book which questions the use of tragic as applied to the plays of Sartre and Camus, and which questions the claim of sociologists and psychologists that *les sciences humaines* are able to render an exact accounting of man. Since Jean-Marie Domenach is today forty-five years old, he was in his twenties when existentialism was exerting the greatest influence in France. Even if at the present time Domenach has moved quite far away from Sartre's philosophy, he cannot refrain from questioning the relationship between existentialism and history. Domenach seems to believe that Sartre's own fidelity to the movement which today has so many adversaries explains his failure to realize the full meaning, the clear stylization of tragedy.

Domenach's book announces a return of the tragic. Not through history or politics, but within man himself. Our age—it is one of its leading characteristics and one for which France has set the example—has a strong liking for philosophy that is essentially tragic. Pascal, Kierkegaard, and Nietzsche are at the source of much of our modern consciousness. At the same time another group of philosophers—Hegel, Marx and Freud—have tried to teach modern man how to rid himself of his illusions and also how to face himself without equivocation. For such a critic as Jean-Marie Domenach, and such a philosopher as Paul Ricoeur, our sense of the tragic is precisely this knowledge of the self.

There are many reflections in Domenach's book on specific literary works and on specific philosophies, but the principal reflections are on himself in order to see what he calls his inner enemy. The tragic reveals to us that the enemy is not outside of us, in the form of a god or nature or fate, but is within us. Domenach would say that the enemy is in a man as long as he does not recognize himself. For an existentialist, our enemies are other people (*les autres*) and they must be expelled from our consciousness, but for Domenach the enemy is within man, and is a being with whom he has to live but who must be discovered.

Domenach characterizes our age as a society of consumption (*société de consommation*) from which man has disappeared. The sense of the "tragic" is the best approach for the restoration of man. He characterizes existentialism as a second romanticism whose logic is based upon the absurd. Both Camus and Sartre were concerned with creating a new humanism and this effort prevented their creating the tragedy that is suitable to the age. *La Chute*, Domenach says, is the only really tragic work of Camus. He recognizes the dramatic elements in the plays of Sartre, but claims they never reach (not even in *Huis clos*) the fullness of tragedy when the conflict takes place within the protagonist in the form of a personal, essential, ontological conflict. He looks upon Sartre as a worthy successor of Victor Hugo, as a Manichean genius. Camus remained closer to the Greek sense of tragedy, accusing the gods (in whom he did not believe) for the woes of humanity.

Tragedy, in its fullest meaning, has for Domenach its center in language. It is the verbal stylization of what is tragic. It has always been the artistic means by which language throws into relief and questions the relationship between man and the gods. Domenach wonders whether the same sense of tragedy can be maintained when language itself is being questioned as that final possibility man has to speak about himself and to communicate his thoughts.

This questioning of the validity of language has been raised by the structuralists, and it is also an important theme of Beckett. One of Beckett's characters says: *Je suis fait de mots . . . des mots des autres*. And in another passage: *Je n'existe pas, le fait est notoire*. After the death of God, announced by Nietzsche, came the death of man, announced by Beckett. The last proof of man's existence is in his speech, but this speech comes to him from the social group. At the end of man's effort to know himself and to rationalize about himself, he comes upon a kind of thinking which is fundamental and collective. This is what Lévi-Strauss calls *la pensée sauvage*. In the plays of Ionesco, Domenach finds that an individual is defined by this mechanical form of thinking, by this erupting of words that come from a distant past and which form, for the critic, the presence of the tragic in the plays.

Thus he believes that the tragic is a permanent element of man's fate, and that when a culture claims it is going to eradicate the tragic, it is exposing itself to a terrifying and avenging return of the tragic. In other words, the tragic is provoked every time a man is motivated by a desire for knowledge, and every time he experiences the desire for freedom. Domenach argues that this form of the tragic is not only inevitable, but beneficent, health-giving. Europe has continued to survive because of it, and has found its fullest vitality in this dialogue of question and answer it carries on with the gods. Contemporary civilization is threatened only when it gives its unqualified adherence to one certainty, to one total explanation, to one all-embracing scheme of values.

Every book that attempts a definition of the tragic and tragedy, attempts too much. Tragedy is the treasure house of those thoughts man has had through the centuries on his freedom and on his guilt. Prometheus is still suffering for us. Oedipus, blinded, is still walking along the roads of the old world and the new world. Each time that Antigone speaks, there is a Creon to answer her and send her to her death. But the term itself of tragedy is impossible to encompass, because it is the picture of man's fate with all of its contradictions and all of its absurdities.

Domenach in his role of critic speaks almost as a prophet when he explains the title of his book by his belief that we have come today to the end of the period of revolutions, that is, the period when the tragic was enacted and lived in real life. This will be followed by a period when tragedy will be performed, when tragedy will return to the stage.

The first volume of Paul Guth's *Histoire de la littérature française* is, in a way, an answer to a question raised by many of the modern French critics: Is literary history possible or how can literary history be written today? The critic is never very far away from the professor, although he usually seems more determined not to bore his public as much as the professor. From the classroom teaching of literature, where so much is based upon the material found in manuals, in such histories as those of Lanson, Bédier and Hazard, Braunschvig, Castex and Surer, Lagarde and Michard, the student retains not much more than a series of pictures, of images that sentimentally are reviewed each year in each succeeding class: Villon looking at the gallows and the charnel house, Montaigne looking up at the beams of his tower library, Ronsard listening to Cassandre Salviati sing in the château de Blois, Voltaire giving a sermon in the church of Ferney, Chateaubriand watching his father walk back and forth after supper in the château de Combourg, Gautier's red vest at the première of *Hernani*, Hugo communing with the spirits on the island of Guernesey, Balzac's coffee pot, Baudelaire's mistress Jeanne, Verlaine's absinth. In addition to such portraits, the student may retain for years a certain number of key phrases, even if their context becomes hazy:

> *la douce France*
> *fais ce que voudras*
> *qui te l'a dit?*
> *cultivons notre jardin*
> *déesse aux yeux bleus*
> *la flèche unique au monde*
> *ce toit tranquille*
> *le petit pan de mur jaune*
> *l'enfer c'est les autres*

These are memories more of the circumstances surrounding literary creation than the creation itself. It does not mean however that in the classroom the other work of literary analysis was neglected. It simply means that the analysis of exterior signs is easier to remember than the analysis of the profound motivation of a text. Lanson himself devoted many of his pages to an analysis of the works. Bédier and Hazard traced the evolution of French sensibility in their history. The successors of Lanson have included in their histories portraits, descriptions of atmosphere, anecdotes, bibliography, as well as critical commentary. Paul Guth, in this newest history of French literature, has retained these elements, but he has changed the tone of his writing by wishing to hold his readers and give them pleasure.

Guth's tone is the opposite of Lanson's dead seriousness. Guth's older readers will not feel they are in school, and his younger readers will learn many fascinating details that are often omitted from classroom discoveries. These details are imparted with such deftness, such gracefulness that they become memorable ornaments in a history of past literary achievements which are always interpreted in the light of the present. Thus the troubadours of the twelfth century bear some resemblance to the *yéyés* of Paris and the beatniks of San Francisco. Froissart of the fourteenth century, usually considered unreadable by non-historians, is described by Guth as the first of our great reporters, as one of our eminent television interviewers. He has the journalist's skill of calling attention to his titles and thereby whetting the appetite of his readers: *Madame de Sévigné, la veuve joyeuse,* and *le Marquis de Sade, victime de sa belle-mère.*

Paul Guth may well displease some of the new critics by expertly analyzing the relationship between Rousseau and Thérèse, and offering very little explanation of *Le Contrat social,* and by omitting from his bibliography Jean Starobinski's important work on Rousseau. Guth states that he belongs neither to the new nor to the old school of criticism, and in fact, almost in justification of this claim, he refers neither to Picard nor to Barthes in his discussion of Racine.

With the development of *les sciences humaines,* which

include sociology, ethnology, economics, psychology, and linguistics, there are new responsibilities not only for the discipline of history, but also for literary criticism and the history of literature. The work of a writer reflects the culture, the taste, the philosophy, and the language of his age. In describing the evolution of language and sensibility, the literary historian has to be concerned with why one author is anchored in the past, and why another author is the prophet of the future, of why Charles d'Orléans is quite purely a poet of the fifteenth century, and why François Villon is a poet of the fifteenth century as well as of the twentieth.

A literary historian has to be open to all schools and all persuasions. Paul Guth's work, which, when the second volume is published, will probably reach twelve hundred pages, comes close to this requirement. It is a synthesis of historical, philosophical, economic, linguistic, and literary knowledge. It reflects also a method of reading in depth key works in French literature which permits this historian-critic to compare works in terms of their structure, their themes, and their style. He moves easily between approaches that are recognizably Sainte-Beuve's and Lanson's to those that are Bachelard's and Proust's.

Bibliography
of works referred to or quoted

Agathon. *L'Esprit de la nouvelle Sorbonne.* 1911
Alain. *Propos de littérature.* 1934
———. *Stendhal.* 1935
Bachelard, Gaston. *La Psychanalyse du feu.* 1937
———. *Lautréamont.* 1939
———. *L'Eau et les rêves.* 1942
———. *L'Air et les songes.* 1943
———. *La Poétique de la rêverie.* 1960
———. *La Poétique de l'espace.* 1957
———. *La Flamme d'une chandelle.* 1961
Barthes, Roland. *Le Degré zéro de l'écriture.* 1953
———. *Michelet par lui-même.* 1954
———. *Mythologies.* 1957
———. *Sur Racine.* 1963
———. *Essais critiques.* 1964
———. *Critique et vérité.* 1966
Bataille, Georges. *L'Expérience intérieure.* 1943
———. *Sur Nietzsche.* 1945
———. *La Part maudite.* 1949
———. *L'Érotisme.* 1957
———. *La Littérature et le mal.* 1957
Baudelaire, Charles. *L'Art romantique.* 1868
Baudouin. *Psychanalyse de l'art.* 1929
———. *Psychanalyse de Victor Hugo.* 1943
Bayle, Pierre. *Dictionnaire historique et critique.* 1697
Béguin, Albert. *L'Ame romantique et le rêve.* 1937
Bellay, J. du. *Défense et illustration de la langue française.* 1549
Bémol, M. *La Methode critique de Valéry.* 1949
Benda, Julien. *Le Bergsonisme ou une philosophie de la mobilité.* 1912

Benda, Julien. *Belphégor*. 1918

———. *La Trahison des clercs*. 1927

———. *La France byzantine*. 1945

———. *Trois idoles romantiques*. 1949

Blanchot, Maurice. *Faux pas*. 1943

———. *La Part du feu*. 1949

———. *Lautréamont et Sade*. 1949

———. *L'Espace Littéraire*. 1955

———. *Le Livre à venir*. 1959

Blin, Georges. *Baudelaire*. 1939

———. *Stendhal*. 1958

Boileau. *L'Art poétique*. 1674

Bonaparte, Marie. *Edgar Poe*. 1933

Bourget, Paul. *Essais de psychologie contemporaine*. 1883

Brasillach, Robert. *Corneille*. 1938

Bremond, Henri. *Histoire littéraire du sentiment religieux en France*. 1916–1931

———. *La Poésie pure*. 1925

———. *Prière et poésie*. 1927

Brombert, Victor. *The Novels of Flaubert: A Study of Themes and Techniques*. 1967

Brunetière, Ferdinand. *L'Evolution de la critique*. 1890

Calvet, Jean. *Renouveau catholique dans la littérature contemporaine*. 1927

Camus, Albert. *Le Mythe de Sisyphe*. 1943

———. *L'Homme révolté*. 1951

Chapelain, Jean. *Les Sentiments de l'Académie française sur "Le Cid."* 1637

Chateaubriand, François-René. *Le Génie du christianisme*. 1802

Claudel, Paul. *Positions et propositions*. 1929

Daniel-Rops. *Notre inquiétude*. 1926

Daudet, Léon. *Le Stupide 19e siècle*. 1926

Domenach, Jean-Marie. *Le Retour du tragique*. 1967

Doubrovski, Serge. *Pourquoi la nouvelle critique?* 1966

Du Bos, Charles. *Approximations*. 7 vols. 1922–1937

———. *Qu'est-ce que la littérature?* 1938

Etiemble. *Hygiène des lettres*. 1952

Foucault, Michel. *Les Mots et les choses*. 1966

France, Anatole. *La Vie littéraire*. 1888–1894

Garaudy, Roger. *D'un réalisme sans rivages*. 1967

Gide, André. *Prétextes*. 1908

———. *Nouveaux prétextes*. 1911

Gide, André. *Incidences*. 1924
———. *Divers*. 1931
———. *Dostoievski*. 1923
———. *Journal des Faux-monnayeurs*. 1926
Glauser, Alfred. *Thibaudet et la critique créatrice*. 1952
Goldmann, Lucien. *Le Dieu caché*. 1956
———. *Pour une sociologie du roman*. 1964
Gourmont, Remy de. *Livres des masques*. 1896–1898
———. *Promenades littéraires*. 1904–1927
Guth, Paul. *Histoire de la littérature française des origines au siècle des lumières*. 1967
Hugo, Victor. *Préface de Cromwell*. 1827
Lacan, Jacques. *Écrits*. 1966
Laforgue, René. *L'Échec de Baudelaire*. 1931
Lanson, Gustave. *Histoire de la littérature française*. 1894
Lasserre, Pierre. *Le Romantisme français*. 1907
Lemaître, Jules. *Les Contemporains*. 1885–1918
Lévi-Strauss, Claude. *Tristes tropiques*. 1955
———. *La pensée sauvage*. 1962
———. *Le Cru et le cuit*, Vol. I of *Mythologiques*. 1964
———. *Du miel aux cendres*, Vol. II of *Mythologiques*. 1967
Malherbe, François de. *Commentaire de Desportes*. 1606
Mallarmé, Stéphane. *Divagations*. 1897
Maritain, Jacques. *Art et scolastique*. 1920
———. *Antimoderne*. 1922
———. *Réponse à Jean Cocteau*. 1926
———. *Frontières de la poésie*. 1935
———. *Situation de la poésie*. 1938
———. *Creative Intuition in Art and Poetry*. 1953
———. *Le Paysan de la Garonne*. 1966
Massis, Henri, *Jugements*. 1923–1924
———. *Au long d'une vie*. 1967
Maulnier, Thierry. *Racine*. 1936
———. *Introduction à la poésie française*. 1939
Mauron, Charles. *Mallarmé l'obscur*. 1941
———. *Introduction à la psychanalyse de Mallarmé*. 1950
———. *L'Inconscient dans l'oeuvre et la vie de Racine*. 1957
———. *Des métaphores obsédantes au mythe personnel*. 1963
Maurras, Charles. *Idée de la critique*. 1896
———. *Les Amants de Venise*. 1902
Mounier, Emmanuel. *Introduction aux existentialismes*. 1947
Paulhan, Jean. *Fleurs de Tarbes*. 1941
———. *Clef de la poésie*. 1945

Péguy, Charles. *Victor-Marie, comte Hugo*. 1910
Picard, Raymond. *Nouvelle critique ou nouvelle imposture?* 1965
Picon, Gaëtan. *Usage de la lecture*. 1960
Poulet, Georges. *Études sur le temps humain*. 1950
———. *La Distance intérieure*. 1952
———. *Les Métamorphoses du cercle*. 1961
———. *L'Espace proustien*. 1963
Proust, Marcel. *Contre Sainte-Beuve*. 1953
Raymond, Marcel. *De Baudelaire au surréalisme*. 1933
Renan, Ernest. *Essais de morale et de critique*. 1859
Richard, J.-P. *Poésie et profondeur*. 1955
———. *Littérature et sensation*. 1954
———. *L'Univers imaginaire de Mallarmé*. 1962
———. *Paysage de Chateaubriand*. 1967
Rivière, Jacques. *Études*. 1912
———. *A la trace de Dieu*. 1925
Rousset, Jean. *La Littérature de l'âge baroque en France*. 1954
———. *Forme et signification*. 1962
Sainte-Beuve. *Les Lundis*. 1849–1862
———. *Port-Royal*. 1840–1859
Sartre, J.-P. *L'Etre et le néant*. 1943
———. *Qu'est-ce que la littérature?* 1947
———. *Baudelaire*. 1947
———. *Saint Genet, comédien et martyr*. 1952
———. *Situations* I (1947), II (1948)
Scaliger, Jules César. *La Poétique*. 1561
Staël, Mme de. *De la littérature*. 1800
Starobinski, Jean. *Montesquieu par lui-même*. 1953
———. *J.-J. Rousseau: La Transparence et l'obstacle*. 1958
———. *L'Oeil vivant*. 1961
Taine, Hippolyte. *Essai sur La Fontaine et ses fables*. 1853
———. *Histoire de la littérature anglaise*. 1864–1869
Thibaudet, Albert. *La Poésie de Stéphane Mallarmé*. 1912, 1926
———. *Flaubert*. 1922
———. *Physiologie de la critique*. 1922
———. *Réflexions sur le roman*. 1938
———. *Histoire de la littérature française depuis 1789*. 1936
Valéry, Paul. *Variété*, 5 vols. 1924–1944
Voltaire. *Théâtre de Corneille avec des commentaires*. 1764
Weber, J.-P. *Genèse de l'oeuvre poétique*. 1960

Index